STUDIES IN ETHICS AND THE PHILOSOPHY OF RELIGION

General Editor: D. Z. Phillips

STUDIES IN ETHICS AND THE PHILOSOPHY OF RELIGION
General Editor: D. Z. Phillips

VOLUME I
The Problem of Evil
by M. B. Ahern

VOLUME II
Moral Reasoning
by R. W. Beardsmore

VOLUME III
Theology and Intelligibility
by Michael Durrant

VOLUME IV
Humanism and Ideology
by James R. Flynn

VOLUME V
The Five Ways:
St. Thomas Aquinas' Proofs of God's Existence
by Anthony Kenny

VOLUME VI
Moral Practices
by D. Z. Phillips and H. O. Mounce

VOLUME VII
God and Timelessness
by Nelson Pike

VOLUME VIII
Without Answers
by Rush Rhees

VOLUME IX
Morality and Purpose
by J. L. Stocks

STUDIES IN ETHICS AND THE PHILOSOPHY OF RELIGION

VOLUME II

Moral Reasoning
By R. W. Beardsmore

LONDON AND NEW YORK

First published in 1969
by Routledge & Kegan Paul Ltd.

Published 2014 by Routledge
2 Park Square, Milton Park, Abingdon, Oxfordshire OX14 4RN

Simultaneously published in the USA and Canada
by Routledge
711 Third Avenue, New York, NY, 10017
First issued in paperback 2014

Routledge is an imprint of the Taylor & Francis Group, an informa business

© R. W. Beardsmore, 1969

All rights reserved. No part of this book may be reprinted or reproduced or utilised in any form or by any electronic, mechanical, or other means, now known or hereafter invented, including photocopying and recording, or in any information storage or retrieval system, without permission in writing from the publishers.

British Library Cataloguing in Publication Data
A catalogue record for this book is available from the British Library

Library of Congress Cataloging in Publication Data
A catalog record has been requested

ISBN 978-0-415-31842-6 (hbk)
ISBN 978-1-138-87126-7 (pbk)

Publisher's Note
The Publisher has gone to great lengths to ensure the quality of this reprint but points out that some imperfections in the original book may be apparent.

STUDIES IN ETHICS AND THE PHILOSOPHY OF RELIGION

The Series is meant to provide an opportunity for philosophical discussions of a limited length which pursue in some detail specific topics in ethics or the philosophy of religion, or topics which belong to both fields. For the most part, the Series will present work by contemporary philosophers. The contributors, while not representing any single philosophical school, will be in sympathy with recent developments in philosophy. Occasionally, however, unpublished material by earlier philosophers, or works of importance which are now out of print, or not easily accessible, will appear in the Series.

D. Z. PHILLIPS

Contents

PREFACE	*page* vii
INTRODUCTION	ix

PART I: MORAL REASONS

1.	R. M. HARE: DEDUCTIVE ARGUMENTS AND RATIONALITY	3
2.	MRS. FOOT: MORAL AND EMPIRICAL CRITERIA	11
3.	THE COMMON ASSUMPTION	24
4.	THE DIVERSITY OF MORAL STANDARDS	37
5.	THE REBEL AND MORAL TRADITIONS	54

PART II: MORAL ARGUMENTS

6.	'IS' AND 'OUGHT'	67
7.	MORAL VIEWPOINTS AND OUR IDEAS OF REALITY	78
8.	FACTS AND 'PURE' FACTS	92
9.	THE POSSIBILITY OF CONFLICTING VALUES	104
10.	AGREEMENT AND MORAL COMMUNICATION	120
	CONCLUSION	135
	BIBLIOGRAPHY	138
	INDEX	141

Preface

Most of this essay was written under the supervision of Mr. H. O. Mounce, and I should like to acknowledge a very great debt to him, both for the benefit of the many discussions which I have had with him and for his detailed criticisms of the essay as a whole.

Acknowledgements are also due to Mr. D. Z. Phillips, who read the manuscript at various stages of completion and made many valuable suggestions, and to Professor J. L. Evans, whose comments on the earlier chapters helped me considerably.

Finally, I should like to thank my wife, Pamela, for her constant help and encouragement. It is to her that this book is dedicated.

R.W.B.

Bangor
November 1968

In considering a different system of ethics there may be a strong temptation to think that what seems to *us* to express the justification of an action must be what really justifies it there, whereas the real reasons are the reasons that are given. These *are* the reasons for or against the action. 'Reason' doesn't always mean the same thing; and in ethics we have to keep from assuming that reasons must really be of a different sort from what they are seen to be.

> Ludwig Wittgenstein: reported by Rush Rhees ('Some Developments in Wittgenstein's View of Ethics')

Introduction

Sometimes when people make moral judgements about the actions, choices, decisions, or character of others, the judgements which they make are disputed. 'Smith', one man remarks, 'is a despicable person'. Someone else disagrees. He has always found Smith to be perfectly upright in his dealings with him. When this happens, each party to the dispute will probably try to defend what he has said by giving reasons. One points out that Smith is always polite, never goes back on his word, and pays his debts; the other claims that Smith tends to ignore people's feelings, is insensitive to suffering, and so on.

It is from situations like these that the issues with which this monograph is concerned arise. For my aim is to bring out what is involved in the processes of reasoning by which men seek to justify their moral judgements.

In some respects this task is similar to that which faces the philosopher in other fields. The philosopher of science, concerned with the types of reasoning by which the scientist reaches his conclusions, those philosophers who turn their attention to ordinary empirical judgements, the philosopher of history and the moral philosopher are, to some extent, presented with similar puzzles to solve and similar confusions to dispel.

Nevertheless, in order to understand the issues with which I am here concerned, it is necessary to realise that moral reasoning (and, to some extent, aesthetic reasoning)

Moral Reasoning

gives rise to difficulties which are peculiar to itself, and which are in some ways more acute than those with which other fields of philosophy are concerned. These are largely due to the nature of the subject-matter with which the moral philosopher deals. For there are important differences between the typical empirical dispute (such as arises in history, science, economics, etc.), and the typical moral (or aesthetic) dispute. Suppose, for instance, that someone tells me that Da Vinci's 'Mona Lisa' has been moved to the Tate Gallery and I disagree. This would, I suppose, be a characteristic empirical disagreement; and the important thing to note is that, although it may be difficult to decide which of us is right, we can at least imagine what would solve the dispute. Though we may disagree in the judgements that we make, both of us agree about what would count as a reason for saying that there was, or was not, a certain painting in the Tate.

On the other hand, in ethical disputes nothing comparable need be true. Often these are not decidable, even in principle, simply because the disputants cannot even agree over what criteria to apply. They each have reasons for the judgements that they make, but neither admits the relevance of the other's reasons. The argument has reached deadlock.

Now, the possibility of this sort of disagreement makes it clear that in morality reasons play a quite different part from elsewhere. Indeed, so great are the differences that in the past philosophers have been tempted to offer analyses of moral judgements, which would rule out the possibility of reasoning in morality, or at least reduce it to some variety of persuasion or propaganda. Thus moral judgements have been compared to statements of likes and dislikes, or to expressions of approval and disapproval. And since people do not normally try to offer reasons for their loathing of carrots or attempt to justify an expression of disgust, such theories may make us feel that reasons play a very minor part, or perhaps no part at all, in moral discourse.

More recently this sort of programme has fallen into

Introduction

disrepute. While recognising the crucial differences between the sort of justifications offered in empirical disputes, and those offered in moral disputes, philosophers have tended to feel that it is their job to give an account of the rules governing the latter, rather than to deny that there are any. Nor is it any part of my purpose here to deny that such an account is necessary. I am concerned only that the account should be the right one. On the other hand, it does seem to me that the majority of contemporary theories offer quite inadequate explanations of moral reasoning. My aim is to explain and rectify these inadequacies.

It is possible to find in the writings of present-day philosophers two main accounts of moral reasoning. Since it often seems to be assumed that we are committed to accepting one or the other of these accounts, and since I believe this assumption to be false, I shall begin by outlining some of the main features of these opposing accounts.

1. The first of the accounts with which we shall be concerned is to be found in its most uncompromising form in the theories of certain Existentialist philosophers, but may also be seen in the writings of philosophers like R. M. Hare,[1] P. H. Nowell-Smith,[2] and K. R. Popper.[3]

One way of seeing what their theory of moral reasoning involves is to consider it in relation to their account of morality in general. Briefly, this rests upon the assumption that moral discourse is to be distinguished from, say, scientific or historical discourse, not by its subject-matter, but by its formal characteristics. Moral judgements are thought to have no subject-matter which is peculiar to themselves. We decide what is to count as a moral judgement, not by looking at *what* is said, but by looking at the *way* in which it is said.

Thus on Hare's account, for instance, we might be justified in saying that a man who claimed that it was wrong to

[1] *The Language of Morals* and *Freedom and Reason*.
[2] *Ethics*.
[3] *The Open Society and Its Enemies*, vol. 1.

shave before midday was not expressing a moral judgement, if we were able to show that he did not regard this judgement as also binding on him. For Hare insists that for something to count as a moral judgement it must apply equally to all people in similar circumstances.[1] But we should not be justified in saying that this was not a moral judgement simply on the grounds that its subject-matter was morally irrelevant. For any judgement, however pointless it may seem, can be counted as a moral judgement provided that it satisfies Hare's formal requirements.

Central to this account of moral judgement as a whole is an account of the nature of moral deliberation. I mentioned earlier that, while there seems to be a general agreement over what counts as a good reason for an empirical belief, this does not seem to apply in the sphere of morality. The account in question, however, insists on even more radical differences. Not only is there no comparable agreement in morality, but indeed what counts as a good reason depends entirely on the individual's choice. Of course, it would be strange, so the doctrine runs, if a man were to criticise people simply because they parted their hair on the right-hand side. But there would be nothing absurd in this. If he were consistent in his criticism, then we should be forced to admit that for him this counted as a reason for moral condemnation. To go on asking, 'But what can the way a man parts his hair have to do with morality?' would, on this account, be a sign of conceptual confusion.

Even allowing that most of its supporters would hedge it round with far more qualifications than I have indicated, I think that this theory is mistaken. For I regard it as mistaken in principle. I shall seek to show that unless it is possible to draw limits – and not merely formal ones – to what can count as a relevant consideration in morality, then it must be conceded that reasoning has no part to play in moral discourse.

2. Though the second account is to be found to some extent in the writings of the earlier utilitarians, its main

[1] *The Language of Morals*, pp. 80–1.

Introduction

contemporary support comes from writers such as G. E. M. Anscombe,[1] P. T. Geach,[2] and Mrs. P. Foot.[3]

Like the account just described, its main aim is to show that moral judgements are open to justification, and in this way to distinguish moral argument from mere persuasion. But, unlike Hare and the Existentialists, its supporters firmly reject the suggestion that the individual is central in deciding what is relevant in moral arguments. On the contrary, for them moral justification is governed by extremely strict rules, rules which are quite independent of personal choice. Sometimes (e.g. occasionally in Mrs. Foot's writings) it is suggested that the relation between reasons and conclusion in a moral argument is one of logical entailment. A man's courage is only a reason for calling him good, if the sentence, 'Though he has courage, he is evil' can be shown to be self-contradictory. Generally a less strict relation is held to obtain. Nevertheless, in both cases moral argument is supposed to be governed by rules which are just as strict as those governing other forms of argument.

Now, if true, this account does undoubtedly show that moral argument is a rational activity. For its standards of rationality will be just the same as those governing other areas of discourse. My main objection to it is that it makes these standards far *too* strict. For it excludes the possibility of the sort of moral disagreement which I described earlier. That is, the sort of disagreement which arises when the disputants differ not only in the judgements which they make, but also in what they count as a reason for these judgements.

In considering the nature of moral reasoning then, we are faced with two conflicting accounts. And these may well seem to present the moral philosopher with a dilemma. Either he accepts that moral reasoning is a realm in which there are no rules at all, or at best only noncommittal, formal ones governing the sort of thing that is to count as a reason. Or he holds that there are rules, but rules so rigid

[1] 'Modern Moral Philosophy.'   [2] 'Good and Evil.'
[3] 'Moral Arguments', 'Moral Beliefs', 'Goodness and Choice'.

that something can count as a reason only if its acceptance logically entails the moral judgement for which it is intended as a reason, or at least commits one to it, regardless of one's moral beliefs.

It is worth noting that the same sort of dilemma is not unknown in other spheres of philosophy. Hume's account of the causal relationship in *An Enquiry Concerning Human Understanding*, for instance, rests on the assumption that there must be either a strict, logically necessary connection between a cause and its effect, or no connection of any kind. In pointing out that there were faults in the rationalist and Lockean accounts of science, according to which the first alternative was held to be true, he believed himself to have shown that anything could be the cause of anything.[1]

Of course, few philosophers nowadays would accept Hume's assumption. Yet in the sphere of ethics very similar assumptions go largely unquestioned. It is the purpose of this essay to show that they must be rejected.

In what follows then, I shall suggest that there is a third alternative which both ignore. To show that this is so, I shall make use of two main lines of argument.

In the first section of this essay I begin by arguing that if moral argument is to be a rational activity, then there must be some rules governing what can count as a relevant consideration. Reasons in morality cannot be just whatever the agent chooses to mention. Nevertheless, I reject the suggestion that these rules are as strict as many philosophers would have us believe. Indeed I try to show that both of the accounts under consideration rest on a mistaken assumption, since both assume that different considerations can count as moral reasons only by virtue of some common property which they all possess. In rejecting this assumption we see that a third account is possible; an account which, while it does not seek to conceal the differences which may exist between men of different beliefs, does allow us to show that morality is rational.

[1] *An Enquiry Concerning Human Understanding*, section vii.

Introduction

In the second section this line of argument is pursued further with an account of the role which reasons play in moral arguments. I show that although it would be wrong to suppose that moral arguments are subject to the same sort of rules as empirical arguments, this does not mean that the agent is free to argue as he chooses. For his arguments can be understood only within the context of certain traditions, within which there are rules for what can count as a good argument.

Before I can begin I should however make one last point. The writings of Hare and Mrs. Foot raise many issues with which I am not here concerned, and which I therefore either ignore completely or consider only indirectly.

In consequence, if this essay is regarded as a scholarly examination of the work of these philosophers, it will inevitably be regarded as inadequate. My excuse is simply that this is not my intention. I am concerned with the theories which Hare and Mrs. Foot offer, only in so far as they illustrate certain tendencies in moral philosophy. I choose them solely because they seem to me to offer the most complete account of these tendencies.

PART I
Moral Reasons

1

R. M. Hare: Deductive Arguments and Rationality

Let us begin by considering the question: Are there any rules governing what is to count as a moral reason? So far I have mentioned two sorts of answer which might be given. That given by Hare says: there are no rules; you yourself decide what sort of considerations are relevant. That given by Mrs. Foot says: the rules are extremely strict ones; the individual has no choice at all as to what is to count as relevant to a moral judgement. Now it seems to me that any account which forces us to say either of these things must be incorrect. But before I put forward my own positive theory, I should like to consider the accounts of Hare and Mrs. Foot in greater detail and try to show what is wrong with them. In this way I can at least protect myself against the charge of knocking down men of straw. I shall begin with Hare's theory.

In both of his books Hare tells us that the purpose of his philosophy is to defend the 'rationality of morals' or to show that morality is 'a rational activity'. Consequently his account allots a place of central importance to the notion of a reason. At the beginning of *Freedom and Reason* for example, he tells us that 'both naturalism and my own view . . . hold that judgements about particular things are made for reasons',[1] and later he goes so far as to say that '"ought" –

[1] *Freedom and Reason*, p. 21.

judgements, strictly speaking, would be being misused if the demand for reasons or grounds were thought of as out of place'.[1] This, I think, would meet with fairly general approval among contemporary philosophers. But some would take strong exception to what he says about the *nature* of moral reasons. His account is implicit in one short passage in *The Language of Morals*, where we are told that:

> There are two factors which may be involved in the making of any decision to do something. . . . They correspond to the major and minor premisses of the Aristotelian practical syllogism. The major premiss is a principle of conduct; the minor premiss is a statement, more or less full, of what we should in fact be doing if we did one or the other of the alternatives open to us. Thus if I decide not to say something because it is false, I am acting on a principle, 'Never (or never under certain conditions) say what is false', and I must know that this, which I am wondering whether to say, is false.[2]

Here Hare is presenting us with a certain picture of the typical moral argument or process of moral deliberation. We are invited to construe it on the model of a syllogism, subject to the normal rules of deductive inference. Thus to take Hare's own example, an argument designed to show that one ought not to make some particular statement (X), might proceed as follows:

>> One ought never to say what is false
>> X is false
> therefore, One ought not to say X

The conclusion of the argument states a moral judgement which the agent makes, or a decision which he has reached; the premisses provide his justification for it.

Now I want to make two points about the theory which Hare offers in this passage, which seem to me to cast serious doubts on its plausibility.

In the first place, we may note that, while in the particular example which Hare chooses the minor premiss is one which most people would regard as relevant to the conclusion, this need not be so. *Whatever* we offered as a minor

[1] *Freedom and Reason*, pp. 36–7.   [2] *The Language of Morals*, p. 56.

R. M. Hare: Deductive Arguments and Rationality

premiss, a valid syllogism could be produced by introducing the appropriate major premiss. Consider, for example, the following argument:

> One ought always to hit one's brother-in-law on Tuesdays
> Today is Tuesday
> therefore, You ought to hit your brother-in-law

Now I do not think that the day of the week would normally be regarded as a relevant reason for engaging in hostilities towards one's relations. But there is no doubt that on Hare's account it could quite easily be so. For the major premiss of the above argument *ensures* its relevance. And the same would go for any reason which we cared to offer.

This is not to say that Hare is completely blind to these consequences of his theory. In the last chapter of *Freedom and Reason*, where he is considering the question of racial conflict, he does point out that on his principles someone may offer as justifying the ill-treatment of other races reasons which many of us would be loth to regard as relevant, e.g. physical characteristics such as the colour of a man's skin or the shape of his nose. (This is so because the argument, 'All people with certain physical characteristics ought to be ill-treated; this man has those characteristics; therefore, this man ought to be ill-treated', is valid.) Hare interprets this as showing that his account of moral justification is not committed to any particular moral standpoint. And this, of course, is true. What Hare does not seem to realise is that, if we accept his account, then there is no consideration, no matter how irrelevant it might seem to be, which could not be regarded as a moral reason. Neutrality is bought at the price of vacuity.

In the second place, I want to draw attention to some of the differences between what Hare accepts as constituting a moral reason, and what we should normally accept. We have seen that he regards moral arguments as processes of syllogistic inference to a moral conclusion, with the premisses providing our reasons for accepting the conclusion. So it is at least clear that he is committed to the view that a statement corresponding to one of his minor premisses could not alone fully justify a moral judgement. (It might, of course, be the only reason *given*, but this could only be because a major premiss had been tacitly assumed, as in the case of an enthymeme.) Hare would not, for instance, accept that to point out that a statement was untrue, could ever be a sufficient reason for asserting that someone ought not to make it. And it seems to me that this conflicts with our ordinary use of the word 'reason'.

To see this, let us consider what might be regarded as a paradigm case of someone making a judgement for a reason. Suppose a woman has to make a choice between telling her husband, who has an incurable disease, the truth about his condition, or deceiving him into thinking that he is suffering from a trivial complaint. (It is this problem with which one of the characters in Tennessee Williams's *Cat on a Hot Tin Roof* is faced.) And suppose, to take the most straightforward case, that she discusses the matter with her family beforehand,[1] and decides that since her husband would prefer to be told the truth, however terrible, she ought not to deceive him. What are we to say about such a case?

Well, two things are clear. (*a*) The decision is a moral one, based on purely moral considerations. Questions of self-interest are irrelevant. (*b*) The wife's reasons are the ones which she gives. This is not to deny that after studying the case a Freudian analyst might come to the conclusion that her real reason was, say, an unconscious hate of her

---

[1] Of course, one's reasons for doing something do not even have to be *thought out* beforehand. The doctor hearing that a patient is seriously ill puts on his hat and coat and goes to him. We should not expect him to compose a mental list of his reasons for doing so – the fact that he is bound by the Hippocratic Oath, or that he has a job to do. If he is a conscientious doctor he will do this only where there is also a good reason for staying where he is, and he is consequently faced with a dilemma, e.g. where he knows the patient in question to be a chronic hypochondriac. I take the case where the reasons are discussed beforehand simply for the sake of clarity.

husband, and the reasons given mere rationalisations. But such a case would necessarily be an exceptional one (which *ex hypothesi* this is not). *All* the reasons we give could not be rationalisations, for the notion of a rationalisation is parasitic upon that of a genuine reason.

Now it seems to me that we should naturally express the wife's reasoning in the above example, as follows:

> My husband would wish me to tell him the truth
> So I ought to tell him the truth

But it is Hare's contention that this way of expressing it is misleading and that in order to rectify this it is necessary to introduce the major premiss, 'One ought always to do what one's husband wishes', and thus bring out the syllogistic form of the argument. It will then be valid 'by the ordinary rules of logic'.[1] The difficulty here is that, while it is possible to turn any non-deductive argument into a syllogism by introducing a major premiss, to do this with moral arguments, or with practical arguments generally, is unilluminating, since the major premiss will often turn out to be one which no one would accept.

To see why Hare's account is unilluminating, let us consider what he would say about the case which I have just mentioned. His contention is that the wife's reasoning requires a major premiss if it is to provide a full justification of her decision. That is to say, her argument should really be represented as:

> One ought always to do what one's husband wishes
> My husband wishes me not to deceive him
> therefore, I ought not to deceive him

The difficulty here is that she would probably deny that she was applying any such major premiss. Indeed it is unlikely (though not impossible) that she would want to commit herself to *any* general statement about what one ought to do in situations where one's husband's wishes are involved. Nor will it do to say (as Hare does in *The Language of*

[1] *The Language of Morals*, p. 48.

Morals[1]) that such a general statement would be only a provisional principle to be modified in the light of experience. Most wives would not feel themselves bound to abide by their husband's wishes if (i) to do so would be harmful to him, or (ii) if he were not *compos mentis*, or (iii) if they were legally separated, or (iv) if he wished them to share their home with his mistress. But it is obvious that these examples do not even begin to exhaust the range of possible exceptions. Nor would any list of examples, however long. It is just possible to think of circumstances in which obeying one's husband's wishes would precipitate China into revolution. But could it be said that a principle which allows for this possibility is more accurate than one which doesn't? Or is there some comprehensive formula which would cover all these evils? Perhaps, but it would be likely to turn our principle into a trivial tautology like 'One ought to obey one's husband's wishes, except where to do so would be wrong'.

Nevertheless, I do not think that it will do merely to say that Hare's premiss is superfluous. For we should then be open to the objection that indeed people *do* say things like 'One ought not to tell lies' or 'One ought to consider one's husband's wishes'. Clearly there is something wrong with an account which holds that 'One ought to tell the truth' is more accurately formulated as 'speak the truth in general, but there are certain *classes* of cases in which this principle does not hold'.[2] 'One ought to tell the truth' is not just a vague generalisation like 'All Frenchmen wear berets', which needs to be qualified by lists of exceptions before it even begins to sound plausible. But if Hare's account is wrong, then what is required is not to banish such moral judgements from the realm of significant discourse, but to give an account of them which will enable us to grasp their function there.

Let us return to the first point which I made about Hare's theory. I said earlier that one of the reasons why Hare thinks that *any* reason might be regarded as relevant to a moral

[1] p. 62. [2] *The Language of Morals*, p. 51.

judgement is that he thinks that it is always possible to introduce some general statement of the form 'One ought to do x' which will ensure its relevance. Now I suggest that there is some truth in this contention. Statements like 'One ought to tell the truth' or 'One ought to consider one's husband's wishes' *do* show the relevance for the reasons we give for moral judgements, only not because, as Hare thinks, they form part of syllogisms which entail these judgements, but because they help to establish the moral context, the framework, within which the reasons are given. Perhaps I can clarify this. Suppose that two people are arguing about whether to report a relative to the police for some fairly minor criminal offence, and that during the argument the one says, 'One ought not to conceal the truth'. Now the purpose of this remark will be to give the other an insight into the range of considerations which he regards as relevant to the case, to give him some idea of the moral attitude that he is adopting. To this the other might reply, 'Well yes, but blood's thicker than water, you know'. And again this remark would help to show the range of considerations which *he* is willing to accept, although here there is less temptation to construe what he says as the major premiss in a syllogism. The first man's remark emphasises the importance of honesty and integrity, and insists that these are the important considerations regardless of who is involved. The second man insists that the demands of the family cannot just be ignored. In both cases what they say does not restrict them to giving any particular reason for the moral judgements they make (as it would if Hare's account were correct), but it does restrict them to giving reasons within a certain range. We should be surprised to hear the second man say, 'So we'll turn him in; after all, you can't go round telling lies to protect scoundrels'.[1]

Now obviously Hare's theory will only be plausible if

[1] It is important to note that I am not suggesting that judgements of the form 'One ought to do x' are always decisive factors in establishing what reasons will be relevant in an argument. I think that Hare's theory overrates their importance in this respect.

statements of the form 'One ought always to do so-and-so' can have any content whatsoever and still remain intelligible. For if this were not so, he would be forced to admit that the reasons we give cannot have just *any* content, for there would be certain reasons which could not be incorporated into a valid syllogism. Hare never considers this possibility because he concentrates on syllogisms whose major premisses *could* function in ordinary discourse, e.g. statements like 'One ought to tell the truth', etc. True he sometimes uses phrases like 'One ought to do x', but these only help the deception. For we tend to think that the variable contained in them could have *any* value, and this is just what is in question.

2
Mrs. Foot: Moral and Empirical Criteria

The *ratio essendi* of Mrs. Foot's work is to be found in the account which I have just been considering. As we have seen, Hare holds a theory according to which there are no limits to what can count as a moral reason, and so far I have tried merely to indicate some of the difficulties into which this leads him. Now, in her articles Mrs. Foot is concerned both to show how Hare's account is wrong and to provide an alternative theory, and it is to this positive theory that I shall now turn my attention, for it seems to be, if anything, less plausible than Hare's own.

I want to begin by asking why it is that Mrs. Foot finds it necessary to advance the sort of theory which we find in 'Moral Arguments', 'Moral Beliefs', and 'Goodness and Choice'. We might be inclined to say that it is simply because she is looking for an alternative to the theory which she has already attacked in her earlier article, 'When is a Principle a Moral Principle?' But while this would be correct as far as it goes, it would be unilluminating, for it neglects many of the deeper issues in the debate between Hare and Mrs. Foot. I suggest that the real answer is to be found at the beginning of 'Moral Arguments', where Mrs. Foot is considering the problem of moral deadlock which I indicated in the Introduction to this essay.[1] As we have seen,

[1] See Introduction, p. x.

this arises because in morals we seem to be continually faced with disputes where agreement cannot be reached, and yet in which the opinions of both parties are equally well-founded. Yet the same does not seem to be true of most other types of disagreement. It is characteristic of, for instance, scientific and empirical disputes that they are always in principle capable of being resolved.[1] If x and y disagree over whether there is a car in the garage, then there is one way in which they can decide the matter once and for all, namely by going and looking. If a and b disagree over the temperature on the Air Ministry roof, then there are recognised ways of finding out who is right. In both cases it would be absurd to say that their views were equally well-founded if they failed to reach agreement. Yet in the sphere of morality the same does not seem always to apply. And this causes difficulties for those for whom the paradigm case of a dispute is an empirical one. Mrs. Foot sums up the problem well when she says, 'How "X is good" can be a well-founded moral judgement, when "X is bad" can be equally well-founded it is not easy to see'.[2]

Now, one way of solving this problem is simply to deny that it exists, that is to deny that such a state of affairs *is* conceivable. And this is in effect what Mrs. Foot does. The reason why empirical disputes are never of the above kind is that there is general agreement about the criteria for deciding them. It is always possible to support an empirical statement with reasons which are both conclusive and whose truth is not disputed by either party. The purpose of Mrs. Foot's later articles is to show that the same is true of moral judgements. That is, she wishes to show that 'it is laid down that some things do, and some things do not, count in favour of a moral conclusion'.[3]

And indeed, if she can establish such a thesis, then the consequences for moral philosophy will be twofold. For not only will she have effectively disposed of Hare's account of

---

[1] I am not ignoring borderline disputes. Here the disagreement *can* be resolved, either by means of further evidence or by some decision about the relevant criteria.   [2] 'Moral Arguments', p. 502.   [3] Ibid., p. 504.

moral reasons, but she will also have provided a procedure for settling *any* ethical dispute. She need only show that there are certain reasons, whose truth is a necessary and sufficient justification of any moral judgement, and she can kill two birds with one stone. We must now see how she intends to accomplish this feat.

In 'Moral Arguments' she begins by considering the word 'rude', which, while perhaps not a paradigm case of a moral term, does at least seem to fall into the class of what Hare would call 'evaluative' terms (of which moral terms are said to form a sub-class). 'It is', she says, 'obvious that there is something else to be said about the word "rude" besides the fact that it expresses fairly mild condemnation; it can only be used where certain descriptions apply.'[1] In the next sentence we are told what the descriptions in question are. A piece of behaviour is rude if and only if it 'causes offence by indicating lack of respect', and whether it does so or not is a purely factual matter.[2] So there are necessary and sufficient conditions of rudeness, and while of course a man may always refuse to discuss 'points of etiquette', once he does agree to do so, he is committed to accepting these as reasons.

Now this is important, for if the range of reasons which we can give for an evaluative judgement is limited in this sort of way, then Mrs. Foot sees no good reason why it should not be limited in the case of moral judgements. We can, she argues, at the very least admit the possibility of this, and it therefore becomes reasonable

> to enquire whether moral terms do lose their meaning when divorced from the pleasure principle, or from some other set of criteria, as the word 'rude' loses its meaning when the criterion of offensiveness is dropped.[3]

---

[1] p. 507.
[2] If I do not directly attack this particular argument, it is because I feel the criticisms of H. O. Mounce and D. Z. Phillips in their article, 'On Morality's Having a Point', to be conclusive. And I should like to take this opportunity of acknowledging a general debt to the point of view proposed in this article.   [3] 'Moral Arguments, p. 510.

Moral Reasoning

What then are this limited set of reasons which alone have any relevance in the justification of our moral decisions and judgements? Well, in 'Moral Beliefs' Mrs. Foot tells us that something can only count as a moral reason if it 'can be shown to be such that it is necessarily connected with what a man wants'.[1] True, other philosophers of the same school have expressed this point in many different ways. Instead of 'What a man wants' Miss Anscombe refers to 'human flourishing',[2] and Mrs. Foot herself sometimes prefers to talk of 'human good and harm'.[3] But the diversity is more apparent than real. For just as a plant flourishes only when its needs are satisfied, so a man is held to flourish only when *his* needs are satisfied. Again, if we are to make some sense of Mrs. Foot's doctrines then 'human good' must be whatever satisfies a man's wants, and by the same token, 'human harm' whatever prevents their satisfaction. Whatever Foot, Anscombe, etc., mean by these various phrases, it is clear that for them it constitutes the point of morality and must therefore provide the sole justification for our moral beliefs.

Now, *prima facie* this would seem to be a most implausible theory. In particular it seems absurd to suggest that the only justification for the virtues of courage, justice, etc., lies in the fact that we need them in our dealings with others, or that only by being just and courageous can a man survive. If justice is only some obscure kind of self-preservation, why do we admire the just man? Is not he, as much as the unjust man, merely looking after himself, only better?

Worse still, Mrs. Foot's theory might well be regarded as a proposal to do away with moral language altogether by reducing it to a variety of straightforward practical language. And indeed, many philosophers of Mrs. Foot's persuasion have openly acknowledged this as their intention. Thus, for instance, in 'Modern Moral Philosophy' Miss Anscombe offers the thesis that 'the concepts of

[1] 'Moral Beliefs', p. 101.   [2] 'Modern Moral Philosophy', p. 18.
[3] e.g. 'Moral Arguments', p. 510.

obligation and duty . . . and of what is *morally* right and wrong, and of the *moral* sense of "ought", ought to be jettisoned, if this is psychologically possible'.[1] Again, G. H. Von Wright, in *The Varieties of Goodness*, has argued that 'the so-called *moral* sense of "good" is a derivative or secondary sense, which must be explained in terms of the non-moral uses of the word',[2] and indeed Mrs. Foot herself raises doubts about whether it makes sense to speak of a moral use of the word 'good'.[3]

Yet we are inclined to say that any attempt to reduce the moral uses of 'good' to a variety of its non-moral uses is bound to end up by misrepresenting the former, for it will necessarily ignore important differences between the two types of judgement in which they occur. I shall try to show that this is what Mrs. Foot's theory in fact does.

Despite its appearance of paradox, Mrs. Foot makes no attempt to support her thesis about moral reasons with any sort of proof in the accepted sense of the word. That it is *possible* that there are reasons which constitute a necessary and sufficient condition for any moral judgement, she does indeed try to establish. That this *is* so, and that these reasons must be of the kind she says, is never proved and Mrs. Foot does not try to prove it. She does, however, offer what Mill might call 'considerations . . . capable of determining the intellect either to give or withhold its assent to the doctrine',[4] and I now want to consider two of these.

The theory that the only considerations relevant to moral judgements are ones connected with 'good and harm' is often thought to be so self-evidently true that it requires no proof.[5] Of course, appeals to self-evidence are generally a rather fruitless method of philosophical argument, but Mrs. Foot's own appeal is of more interest than most, for it

---

[1] 'Modern Moral Philosophy', p. 1.
[2] *The Varieties of Goodness*, p. 1.   [3] 'Moral Beliefs', p. 92.
[4] *Utilitarianism*, p. 7.
[5] If, by 'good and harm', Mrs. Foot meant 'moral good and harm', then what she says *would* be self-evident. But only at the price of becoming trivial. As I have said, this is not what she means.

Moral Reasoning

points to some of the confusions underlying her theory. She says:

> I do not know what could be meant by saying that it was someone's duty to do something, unless there was an attempt to show why it mattered if this sort of thing was not done. How can questions such as 'What does it matter?', 'What harm does it do?', 'What advantage is there in . . . ?', 'Why is it important?' be set aside here?[1]

I suggest that there is a radical confusion in this passage, which becomes apparent if we consider the following example:

Suppose I say to my young son John, 'You know, you ought to be more obedient', and am challenged by Mrs. Foot to give reasons for this assertion. There are two senses in which the reasons which I give might be said to show why John's obedience is important:

1. In one sense my reasons *must* show this, for in this sense to admit that it was not important ('did not matter', 'had no point') would be to admit the triviality of my remark. And no one can regard his own moral judgements as trivial, for a man's morality *is* those sorts of things which he regards as important in his life. 'You ought to do this, but it doesn't really matter whether you do it or not', is a piece of nonsense.

2. In the second sense of 'important', what Mrs. Foot says seems to me to be quite incorrect. We see what this sense is, if we consider the role which the word has in sentences like the following:

(*a*) It is important to clean the machine before use.
(*b*) Important. Light blue touch-paper and retire immediately.
(*c*) It is important to keep on friendly terms with the boss.

In contexts like these, we *do* show how something is important by giving reasons which link it with 'human good and harm' or with the advantage which it is likely to bring. But I do not think that this is the sense in which it is normally used in moral contexts. Indeed, one is inclined to

[1] 'Moral Arguments', p. 510.

Mrs. Foot: Moral and Empirical Criteria

say that if I do try to show how a judgement is important in this sense, then this is an indication that the judgement is not a moral one. For instance, if, in the above example, I were to answer Mrs. Foot by saying, 'If John isn't obedient then he'll soon find out why he ought to be', or 'Because he's beginning to get on my nerves', this would surely be a sign that moral issues were not involved. A reason which was necessarily connected with what a man wants, far from being a paradigm case of a moral reason, as Mrs. Foot thinks, would serve to change the whole character of the discussion. And this is even more obvious if we take her own example of justice. For it is clear that if someone were to recommend justice on the ground that 'You really can't get along without it', we should hesitate to call this a moral belief at all.

Mrs. Foot is, of course, right to say that it must always be possible to support a practical judgement with reasons in terms of 'good and harm' or 'advantage'. For it is reasons of this sort which give what we say its meaning. When I say, 'You ought to water that plant', this would be incomprehensible unless it were understood that plants die without water. But if I am asked to support a moral judgement in this way, then I am at a loss to know what is wanted. As Rush Rhees asks, 'What more could I tell you?'[1]

Now it seems to me that it is only because she conflates these two senses of 'important' that Mrs. Foot's theory has any plausibility. If we do not notice the confusion, we seem to be faced with a dilemma. For while we naturally regard our moral judgements as anything but trivial, and would never admit that they do not really matter, we feel reservations about accepting Mrs. Foot's theory. Yet the passage which I have been considering gives the impression that the only alternatives are (*a*) to give reasons which will show the point of a pointless belief, or (*b*) to accept that her account of moral reasons is correct. The difficulty only disappears when we realise that Mrs. Foot's seemingly impossible task rests on a straightforward confusion of two

[1] 'Some Developments in Wittgenstein's View of Ethics', p. 19.

Moral Reasoning

senses of 'having a point'. In one sense morality is necessarily pointless. In the other it can never be.

I want now to turn my attention to another line of argument which is sometimes used in support of the sort of theory under consideration. It is to be found in Geach's article 'Good and Evil', but Mrs. Foot provides perhaps the most convincing exposition in her 'Goodness and Choice'. Since it seems to pinpoint the fundamental fallacies in the whole approach, I shall briefly summarise the argument before attempting to criticise it. Mrs. Foot's aim is to show that the criteria of goodness of an object are 'always determined and not a matter for decision',[1] and she thinks that this can be done in the following way.

She begins by drawing attention to a class of words which, when preceded by 'good' yield criteria of goodness. The reason why this is so, is that these words (generally referred to as 'functional' words) 'name an object in respect of its function'.[2] For example, the function of a knife is to cut. So it will be a minimum qualification of something being a good knife that it cuts well. If asked why a particular knife is a good one, my reasons must at least refer to the fact that it performs its function well. But, it is argued, we can generalise this point to include words which are not functional in any normal sense of the word. For example, it would be straining language to say that a farmer, a horserider, a book, or a father had a function, yet there is still a limited range of reasons which can be given for commending any one of these. A man can only be a good farmer 'because of his farming, while what counts as good farming must be, e.g., maintaining crops and herds in healthy condition'.[3] Again, 'the minimum condition of good riding is an ability to control a horse',[4] a good book must 'interest us profoundly',[5] and a good father is one who 'looks after his children as best he can'.[6]

[1] 'Goodness and Choice', p. 47.   [2] Ibid.
[3] Ibid., p. 49.   [4] Ibid., p. 50.
[5] Ibid., p. 52.   [6] Ibid., p. 50.

Mrs. Foot: Moral and Empirical Criteria

Now what conclusions can be drawn from all this? Well, Hare had argued that there are no limitations to what can count as a moral reason. Mrs. Foot, by sheer proliferation of examples, seeks to show that this is not true of any of the uses of 'good' outside morals. The conclusion drawn is that if Hare's account were correct with regard to the characteristically moral uses of the term, then these would 'seem to be different from all other cases in which we talk of a good such-and-such'.[1]

Part of the difficulty in criticising this argument is that it is not quite clear what is supposed to be so dubious about this.[2] After all, we *expect* the moral uses of words to differ from their non-moral uses. It would be rather surprising if they did not. But I want to ignore this point. What I want to suggest is that Mrs. Foot has not even established her thesis in the case of the non-moral uses of 'good'. Nor do I think that any such thesis can be established.

Let us see why it is that there are certain cases where the reasons we can give for commending an object are limited. It seems to me that this is because the object in question has a characteristic purpose or point. The generally accepted point of farming is, as Mrs. Foot says, the maintaining of crops and herds in healthy condition. So the minimum qualification for being a good farmer is that one's crops and herds do not die. But it follows from this that if there were disagreement over the point of farming, or if its point were different, then we could no longer necessarily offer this as a reason for saying that someone was a good farmer. If I ask why Jones is a good sewage-farmer, I hardly expect to hear that herds thrive on his land.

Now this is important, for it means that there can be

[1] 'Goodness and Choice', p. 47.

[2] A similar difficulty is presented by Aristotle's rhetorical question, 'Are we then to suppose that, while the carpenter and the shoemaker have definite functions or businesses belonging to them, man as such has none?' (*Nichomachean Ethics*, I, vii, 11). Here we are also inclined to ask, 'Why should this not be so?' Both Mrs. Foot and Aristotle just *assume* that it makes sense to speak of morality and moral agents in the same terms as riding and horse-riders, or carpentry and carpenters.

Moral Reasoning

established criteria by which to settle disagreements, only where an object or activity has some undisputed point. And this does not seem to be the case even outside morality, as becomes apparent when we turn to what Mrs. Foot says about works of art on pp. 52–3 of 'Goodness and Choice'.

'We cannot', she says, 'consider the criteria of goodness in books and pictures without noticing the part which literature and art play in a civilisation such as ours.' Now this, of course, is true, for it is the part which something plays in a civilisation which determines what the criteria *are*. But the reason why Mrs. Foot's argument seems so strange is that, while we cannot imagine any dispute about the purpose of a knife, it is obvious that disputes about the point of works of art do constantly occur.

For example, when Brecht's play *Mann ist Mann* was first staged in Germany, many critics objected to the performance of Peter Lorre on the grounds that it was wooden, unemotional and monotonous. Yet Brecht in his reply to Lorre's critics made it clear that he regarded these qualities as virtues.[1]

How could such a situation arise? The answer seems to be that both had different conceptions of the point of the theatre. According to the traditional concept of the theatre in Germany, the actor tried to make the audience experience the feelings and emotions of the character whom he was playing. He 'lived his part'. But, for Brecht, the theatre had a different purpose. It was intended to appeal less to the spectator's feelings than to his reason.[2]

Because of this, Brecht and his critics reached different conclusions. By traditional standards, Lorre had given a mediocre performance. Yet for Brecht, Lorre's acting was good *precisely because* it was wooden and unemotional.

Now, surely examples like these show the futility of attempting to base any sort of aesthetic criticism on the

---

[1] See B. Brecht, 'Anmerkungen zum Lustspiel "Mann Ist Mann"' in *Schriften zum Theater*, vol. II, especially pp. 73–80.

[2] See, for instance, his remarks in 'Uber eine nicht-aristotelische Dramatik' in *Schriften zum Theater*, vol. III.

Mrs. Foot: Moral and Empirical Criteria

alleged purpose of a work of art. Mrs. Foot's thesis is, no doubt, an illuminating one when restricted to activities which do have a clear-cut, non-controversial point; it is particularly illuminating when applied to games, where the whole activity is directed towards some agreed end, such as scoring a goal or winning a trick. But it would be wrong to assume that even all non-moral activities were of this sort.

But now, what are we to say about morality itself? Do all our moral decisions have some common, undisputed point, such that we can say with certainty what reasons will count as relevant to any moral judgement, as Mrs. Foot thinks?

It seems to me that it is here that the theory under consideration really breaks down. For it is surely *quite* implausible to suggest any one point for all moral action. True there are a host of candidates for this role: 'human good and harm', 'what all men want', 'human flourishing', as well as such traditional stand-bys as 'happiness', 'pleasure', and 'self-interest'. But the majority of these suffer from being either too narrow, like 'pleasure', or too vague, like 'human flourishing'.[1] Now part of the value of Mrs. Foot's work is that she tries to say in precise terms what is involved in conceptions like these. The arguments in 'Moral Beliefs' make it quite clear that for her, human flourishing or human good consists at least in freedom from physical injury. This is why she thinks it possible to impose strict limits on what is to count as a moral reason. If I wish to give a reason why someone ought to do x, I can do so by showing that x leads to something which he wants. And what all men want is to escape injury. So to say that some action will lead to injury is to give a reason for not doing it. It may not always be a conclusive reason, but at least it is always a reason.

The question is, then, whether the fact that some action will lead to injury is always *a* reason for avoiding that action. I think that it is not. We have no difficulty in imagining the

---

[1] For an example of the latter fault, see Miss Anscombe's article 'Modern Moral Philosophy', where, after arguing that the fundamental concept in moral philosophy is that of 'human flourishing', she admits that she is unable to give any precise account of what 'human flourishing' is.

21

kind of person for whom questions about the possible injury resulting from a proposed course of action are quite irrelevant to whether they ought to do it or not. The Jehovah's Witness, refusing to allow a blood transfusion for his dying child, is quite aware of the injuries which may result from his decision. It is just that, for him, such matters have no relevance. Again, consider the following passage from Malcolm's memoir of Wittgenstein:

> Moore's health was quite good in 1946-47, but before that he had suffered a stroke and his doctor had advised that he should not become greatly excited or fatigued. Mrs. Moore enforced this by not allowing Moore to have a philosophical discussion with anyone for longer than one hour and a half. Wittgenstein was extremely vexed by this regulation. He believed that Moore should not be supervised by his wife. He should discuss as long as he liked. If he became excited or tired and had a stroke and died – well, that would be a decent way to die: with his boots on. Wittgenstein felt that ... a human being should do the thing for which he has a talent with all his energy his life long and should never relax his devotion to his job merely in order to prolong his existence.[1]

It seems to me that here Malcolm is not portraying a man for whom philosophy was so important that any injury which might result from it would recede into *relative* insignificance, but rather someone for whom any personal injury done by his life's work would be quite irrelevant. It was not just that, for Wittgenstein, the possible loss of one's life was not an overriding reason for 'taking it easy', but that, for him, it was not a reason at all. Any appeal to 'human good and harm' would have cut no ice at all with Wittgenstein, for as far as he was concerned 'dying with one's boots on' did not count as harm. In the face of cases like these we must surely conclude that the concept of 'what all men want' is an empty one.

It does not, however, follow that all of Mrs. Foot's argument is equally futile. Certainly her positive thesis is not a convincing one, and I think that any attempt to confine moral reasons within the scope of a simple formula would

[1] *Wittgenstein: A Memoir*, pp. 67-8.

be equally unconvincing. It is my purpose to show that the reasons we give for moral judgements are limited in a quite different way. But it is to her credit that she saw the absurdity in Hare's suggestion that anything can count as a moral reason. Her mistake was to assume that the only alternative was that there must be some simple and strict formula governing what could do so. In the following chapter I shall try to show that there is a third alternative, which will allow us to rectify the faults in both theories.

3
The Common Assumption

The aim of this essay is to bring to light and criticise an assumption which underlies many of the debates in modern moral philosophy. I have taken as representative of these debates the recent controversy between Hare and Mrs. Foot, but until now I have contented myself with indicating certain deficiencies in their accounts. We must now consider whether there is not some other account which escapes these criticisms.

In this connection F. P. Ramsey once made an important observation. In a paper called 'Universals' he said:

> In such cases it is an heuristic maxim that the truth lies not in one of the disputed views, but in some third possibility which can only be discovered by rejecting something assumed as obvious by one of the disputants.[1]

Now I suggest that there certainly is at least one false assumption which both Hare and Mrs. Foot make. Both seem to take it for granted that the only way in which we can decide whether something is to count as a moral reason, is first to discover some characteristic common and peculiar to all the manifold instances of moral reasons, and then to examine the particular instance to see whether it possesses this characteristic.

Of course, this assumption is by no means limited to the sphere of moral philosophy. Since the time of Socrates it has

---
[1] *The Foundations of Mathematics*, p. 116–17.

The Common Assumption

been responsible for a great deal of fruitless controversy throughout the whole of philosophy. Nor is its widespread acceptance altogether incomprehensible. After all, in a great many cases where we have to decide whether some object falls into a certain category, the discovery that it possesses or lacks some typical property will enable us to reach a conclusion. Thus we decide what counts as gold by seeing what possesses the property common to all gold of dissolving in aqua regia; we can tell whether something is a mammal by finding out whether it suckles its young; if something does not have gills, then it cannot be a fish, and so on. Nevertheless, in the vast majority of cases the assumption that there must be something common to all instances falling under a general term seems to be wrong, and I want to argue that in moral philosophy the doctrine is a particularly pernicious one.

It is not, however, *prima facie* clear that Hare and Mrs. Foot do make this particular assumption, and I shall begin by defending my contention that they do. Let us consider Hare's account first. Here the matter is complicated by the fact that Hare often criticises others for just the mistake that I am attributing to him, and this might incline us to think that he himself avoids it. A typical passage occurs in chapter 6 of *The Language of Morals*. Hare is considering the view that what justifies our applying the word 'good' to objects of widely different classes is some common factor which they all possess, and he says of the attempt to discover this factor that it

> seems at first sight a natural procedure; for if the use of the word 'good' is common to all classes of objects, it must have a common meaning, and it is natural to suppose that if it has a common meaning there is a common property to which it refers, like 'red'.[1]

But he goes on to say that 'such efforts are doomed to failure'.

Clearly Hare is right. It should be obvious that there can be no common factor in all the different things that we call

[1] *The Language of Morals*, p. 97.

good. (Would it even make sense to say that there was anything common to both the Good Samaritan and a good mackintosh?) Further, the search for a common factor is doomed to failure even in the case where Hare thinks that it has most plausibility, that of colour-words. For there is certainly nothing common to all the things that we call red – light red, dark red, etc. – nothing, that is, beyond the fact that we use the word 'red' to refer to all of them.

Unfortunately, when Hare comes to offer his own positive theory, it is characterised by just the same assumption that he has criticised in the above passage. True, he does not suggest that there is anything common to all the criteria which justify the application of the word 'good'. He thinks that this is unnecessary, for on his theory these only account for *one* of the elements in the word's meaning, the descriptive element. But Hare claims to find another element, the evaluative or commendatory element, which *is* common to all uses of the word.

> I maintain that the meaning which is common to all the instances of the word's use cannot be descriptive and that this common meaning is to be sought in the evaluative (commendatory) function of the word.[1]

Now this clearly commits Hare to the assumption that he earlier criticised. Hare thinks that there are (to some extent) rules governing the use of the word 'good', because he believes himself to have discovered some element (commendation) common to the many situations in which we call things good, and his account of moral reasons follows directly from this assumption. He thinks that there are no rules governing what can count as a moral reason simply because, as we have seen, he is unable to find anything common to all the possible criteria of goodness in different classes of objects. What I am arguing is that the search should never have been begun, since its outcome is irrelevant to the question whether there are such rules.

Let us now turn to Mrs. Foot. Little argument is required

---

[1] 'Geach: Good and Evil', pp. 106–7.

to show that she accepts the same assumption as Hare. For, as I have already shown, she believes that the different types of consideration with which we attempt to justify our moral judgements do have some common element in that they are all connected with human wants. Again, in 'Goodness and Choice' she quite explicitly accepts the analogous assumption about the word 'good'. Criticising Hare's assumption that there is a connection between calling something good and choosing that object, she says:

> Only someone in the grip of a theory would insist that when we speak of a good root we commit ourselves in some way to choosing a root like that. Nor do we need to look for such a connection in order to find out what is common to the different cases where we apply the word.[1]

What is common is simply that all good things are 'of the kind to perform their function well'.[2]

We now begin to see how both of the above accounts draw their life from one basic assumption about the rules governing what counts as a moral reason. Naturally, if we accept this assumption, then in rejecting Hare's theory we shall tend to find ourselves impaled on the other horn of the dilemma, and press-ganged into a fruitless search for some property common to all moral reasons. And if we reject Mrs. Foot's account, we shall be forced to the conclusion that the giving of reasons in morality is a rather arbitrary affair. But there is a way to escape this dilemma. We must deny the presuppositions upon which both arguments trade. This is what I wish to do. And I think that it can best be done by showing just what is wrong with the thesis that Hare offers, and by showing how this can be done without having to accept Mrs. Foot's theory.

As we have seen, despite his insistence on the rationality of morals, Hare is really committed to an account, according to which it is a quite arbitrary matter what is counted as a moral reason. Now it seems to me that this is an absurd doctrine, and one way in which to bring out its absurdity is

[1] 'Goodness and Choice', pp. 58–9.   [2] Ibid., p. 59.

Moral Reasoning

to try to describe some situation of which it might be a true account. If this is unsuccessful, then there will be less temptation to accept Hare's theory.

Now here we are fortunate. For Hare provides us with what might at first sight seem a good example of such a situation. It occurs in chapter 6 of *The Language of Morals*, and while admittedly not drawn from the sphere of morality is clearly thought to be relevant to it. Hare invites us to consider the following case:

> Suppose that someone starts collecting cacti for the first time and puts one on his mantelpiece – the only cactus in the country. Suppose then that a friend . . . sends for one from wherever they grow, and puts it on his mantelpiece, and when his friend comes in, he says, 'I've got a better cactus than yours.'[1]

Now, *ex hypothesi*, neither of Hare's cactus-collectors (let us call the first 'x' and his friend 'y') has any idea of what the criteria of goodness in cacti are. And for this reason I should be disinclined to say that y was using the word 'good' (or 'better') intelligibly. But clearly Hare thinks that he is. Moreover he goes on to say, 'He and his friend may dispute about the criteria of good cacti'.[2]

Here we have what, if Hare's account is to be accepted, should be a quite familiar situation. At first there are no criteria by which to judge a particular set of objects (in this case, cacti). Later, however, these objects begin to play a part in the life of a society and men begin to *set up* criteria. But in doing so they are bound by no rules. They *decide* for themselves what is to count as a relevant reason for saying that a cactus, or what-have-you, is good.

It is here that the weaknesses of Hare's theory become apparent. For the situation which he has described is certainly not a familiar one, as it should be on his principles. Indeed it is by no means clear that his description is even intelligible. For what could it mean to say that we decide the criteria for calling a cactus good? Suppose, for instance, that x had said that his cactus was good because it had 63 spines

[1] *The Language of Morals*, pp. 96–7.   [2] Ibid., p. 97.

The Common Assumption

and y that *his* was good because it had 27. Is this supposed to be intelligible *as it stands*? Or if someone is perhaps inclined to think that this does have a meaning for us, let them suppose that x had said that his cactus was good because it had been crushed in transit. Would it make sense to maintain that this was relevant? Would we understand what they were saying, without further explanation? Obviously not.

Let us see why this is so. I suggest that at least one of the functions of a reason is to render a person's judgement intelligible, to explain it. And I suggest that what a man says or does is explained when it is shown to exhibit some kind of pattern. This can be seen if we consider an example where an action (rather than a judgement) is explained by someone giving a reason.

In Camus' novel *The Outsider* a young clerk, Meursault kills an Arab. The crime bears many of the marks of a wilful murder; Meursault fires five shots quite deliberately, even though death is caused by the first bullet, and so on. Yet the crime seems unintelligible, for Meursault has no motive for murder and seems to have no personal feelings towards the Arab, or, for that matter, towards anyone. Suppose, however, that he had given a reason for his action, for example, by admitting that he regarded Arabs as an inferior people who should be exterminated. We should now begin to understand the crime and part of this understanding would consist not merely in knowing that Meursault regarded some *particular* reason as relevant, but in being able to fit his action into some sort of context or background, where there are rules governing what is to count as a relevant consideration. We should have been able tentatively to class Meursault along with people like the Nazis and Ku Klux Klan. And this would have helped us to say the sorts of things which he would have been likely to do, and the sort of reasons for which he would have been likely to murder again.

Now when x says that his cactus is a good one because it has been crushed in transit, we are unable to fit what he says into any sort of context. Consequently, although we know that he regards this particular feature as a reason for valuing a cactus, that is all that we do know. We have no idea what else he would regard as relevant, nor do we have any idea what he would regard as irrelevant. And this, of course, is just nonsense. If anything could count as a reason, then there would be no point in offering anything as a reason. (Just as, if anything could count as a Jersey cow, it would tell us nothing to be told that Daisy was a Jersey.) The notion of an arbitrarily chosen reason is a chimera.

Here, however, an objection might be raised. For it might be felt that, although what I have said is true, Hare himself recognises its truth and takes steps to forestall such objections to his theory. There would seem to be some support for such a criticism. For instance, in *Freedom and Reason* he tells us that 'the notion of a reason ... brings with it the notion of a rule, which lays down that something is a reason for something else'.[1] Perhaps then it might be said that I have misrepresented Hare throughout. Perhaps he is *not* committed to the erroneous thesis that moral reasons may be chosen arbitrarily.

I suggest that the answer to this objection is that, while Hare does recognise the importance of rules or standards in morality, he gives a faulty account of the role which they have there. As I pointed out earlier, for him a standard takes the form of a major premiss in a syllogistic argument. Clearly this is not any purely verbal slip. Rather it is a central principle of his doctrine. Hare consistently uses 'rule' or 'standard' and 'major premiss' interchangeably. Thus, for example, on p. 111 of *The Language of Morals* he refers to the 'standard of goodness in strawberries' as a major premiss (presumably of the form 'all strawberries with such-and-such characteristics are good ones'), throughout chapter 4 the standards of good driving are treated as if they were a series of complex major premisses, and so on.

Now this sort of account tempts us into a really radical confusion. For when Hare invites us to regard a standard as a major premiss or as a sort of general statement, we are

[1] *Freedom and Reason*, p. 21.

The Common Assumption

given the impression that just as it is I who decide the content of the statements that I make, so I might also decide the content of the standards which I accept. This sort of assumption is seen quite clearly in the work of Karl Popper, a philosopher often quoted with approval by those who adopt a similar approach to Hare. In *The Open Society*, Popper tells us that the doctrine which he supports maintains that

> norms and normative laws can be made and changed by man, more especially by a decision or convention to observe or alter them, and that it is therefore man who is morally responsible for them.

He goes on:

> these standards are of our making in the sense that our decision to adopt them is our own decision, and that we alone carry the responsibility for adopting them. . . . It is we who impose our standards upon nature, and in this way introduce morals into the natural world.[1]

Now it seems to me that this approach is open to at least two serious objections.

1. In the first place, while it makes perfectly good sense to talk of someone having decided to watch television or go to the pub, or of his having been forced to decide between doing his duty or taking the easy way out, I think that we should be less willing to talk of someone having decided that murder is an evil, for example, or of his having adopted this as his standard. We should not know what to make of someone who talked as if the content of moral laws were dependent on the individual will in this sort of way.

2. But there is an even more telling objection to this sort of theory. As we have seen, the notion of an arbitrarily chosen reason is an absurd one. Now Hare sees this, and in order to escape the charge of arbitrariness to which his account is open, he introduces a reference to standards. But does this really help his case? Surely, on his own account it is still an arbitrary matter what is to count as a standard. The agent creates his own standards by resolving to accept

[1] *The Open Society*, vol. 1, p. 61.

certain considerations as relevant. And this removes one paradox only to substitute another. If, as is alleged, it is we who impose our standards on nature, then for us to make any appeal to those standards would seem to be a rather futile performance.

Similar confusions occur in Hare's account of 'ways of life' on pp. 68–9 of *The Language of Morals*. Here again it is, no doubt, important to recognise that rules and standards only make sense within a way of life. But this point is obscured by Hare's account:

> If pressed to justify a decision completely, we have to give a complete specification of the way of life of which it is a part. This complete specification is impossible in practice to give. ... Suppose, however, that we can give it. If the enquirer still goes on asking, 'But why *should* I live like that?' then there is no further answer to give him.... We can only ask him to make up his mind which way he ought to live; for in the end everything rests on such a decision of principle. He has to decide whether to accept the way of life or not. ...

It is quite easy to see that the statements which Hare makes in this passage are the natural outcome of the particular account of moral reasoning which he offers us. According to this account, one justifies a particular moral judgement by pointing to the major premiss which covers such a situation. One may justify this premiss by an appeal to a still more general one. But the process must have an end, and it ends when one has given a complete specification of a way of life, that is to say when one has stated the most general major premiss which *can* be given. It is then up to the individual whether or not he accepts this.

But does it really make sense to suppose that a person's whole way of life might be based on the sort of decision which Hare describes in this passage? I do not think that it does. The reason why this is so is that it is only *within* a way of life that any decision can be meaningful. It makes sense to speak of a decision to adopt a particular way of life, only within the context of a wider way of life.

The Common Assumption

This becomes clear if we ask why it is that we regard certain decisions as meaningless, even though the sentences used to express them are grammatically legitimate. Why, for example, would it be unintelligible for me to say that I had decided to become the Roman Emperor Caligula. The answer is that, whatever strange things I might do, like ordering people to worship me, or naming my horse 'Incitatus', no one would say that I had decided to become Caligula, simply because in most contexts nothing would count as making such a decision. Of course, this is not to deny that we might think of contexts in which such a decision would be possible. Suppose, for instance, that I had been offered a part in the film production of Robert Graves' *I, Claudius*. I might refuse this offer with the words, 'No, I've decided to be Caligula or nothing at all'.

The same considerations are important when we turn to the sphere of morality. Here again not all decisions are intelligible. We should understand someone who said that he had decided to try to become a better person, but not someone who said that he had decided to commit *hara kiri*. For the institution of *hara kiri* played a part in a feudal Japanese society, which it could not play in twentieth-century Britain.

Thus it is only in terms of certain features of the situation in which it is taken that any decision can be intelligible. Both of the particular decisions considered above were unintelligible because there were no considerations in terms of which they could be explained, even though in other situations, other contexts, such considerations might be found. The difficulty is that in the situation which Hare describes, where it is not a particular course of action, but a whole way of life which is being chosen, all such considerations would of necessity be absent. Whatever decision were made, it could have no relation to the facts of the situation in which it was made. For on Hare's account the only connection which there can be between facts and decisions is a syllogistic one. And any syllogism would require a major premiss which, since a way of life is the ultimate major premiss, cannot be supplied here. Such a decision would therefore be a literally senseless act.

We see then that Hare's account of the rules which govern what is to count as a moral reason will not do. For him it is a sufficient condition of something counting as a moral reason that someone should consistently appeal to that sort of thing in supporting his judgements. What I have tried to show is that this makes nonsense of the idea of a rule. While consistency may be a necessary condition, it is certainly not a sufficient one.

But, for all this, I do not think that Hare's theory is all that far from the truth. I said that one of the functions of a reason is that it should make a judgement intelligible. Now, as we have seen, an arbitrarily chosen reason will not do this. Nor does it make any fundamental difference to point out that the agent continually gives or accepts such considerations as reasons. But suppose that we are able to show that these considerations have connections with the *kind* of things that people accept. Then I think that we should want to say that they were reasons. This shows why Hare's theory is so nearly correct. Certain things count as reasons for me not, as he thinks, because they are the sort of things to which I consistently appeal, but because they are the sort of things which I and others have been brought up to appeal to and accept within some social context.

Let us now return to the case of the cactus. I said that it would not be intelligible if x were to say that his cactus was good because it had been crushed in transit. This is because this characteristic has no connection at all with the sort of things which we normally accept as criteria of goodness in plants. But it would surely have been intelligible if Hare's cactus-lover had said that his cactus was better because of its size. For this has certain similarities to the things which we normally accept as criteria: think of prize blooms, marrows or hothouse peaches. Or he might have said that his cactus had brighter colours (like roses or tomatoes) or luxuriant growth (like honeysuckle or tradescantia) or sound roots (like apple trees). But as for a plant

The Common Assumption

being crushed in transit, this seems to have no connection at all with the normal criteria of goodness in plants, and this is why we are inclined to say that it could not be a criterion here.

It is, however, important to guard against an error. I am not, of course, denying that we might, if we wished, think of situations in which this sort of thing would be regarded as the feature which made an object valuable. To see this, we need only consider stamp-collecting, where defects may actually increase the value of a stamp, by increasing its scarcity. (Although, even here not *any* defect will do: a stamp's value does not increase if it is torn or soiled; it decreases.) So if we were to ask our collector what was good about crushed cacti, and he were to say, 'Oh, their scarcity value', we might begin to understand. We should realise that, however mistakenly, he sees his cactus in the same way that others see Meissen porcelain or Faberge jewellery. But we should not expect him to answer, 'Anything can count as a reason for calling something good, and I regard its being crushed as a reason', for this would be nonsense. And the fact that he is required to give an explanation shows that this is an exceptional case. Generally, when someone gives a reason we recognise it as such without explanation. Here we do not.

The point which I am trying to make is that although it is not possible to exclude *a priori* any feature of an object as a possible criterion of its goodness, we *can* say that if anything is to count as a criterion, then it must in principle be possible to see some relationship between it and the other things which count as criteria of goodness.

True, it may not, as a matter of fact, be possible for us always to explain this relationship. Where, for example, we are dealing with members of a society distant in time from our own, we may simply lack the historical background necessary for an understanding of their beliefs, even though, because of their sincerity and the obvious importance which they attach to certain things, we may not wish to deny that moral considerations are involved.[1] Nevertheless, it must be conceivable that a background should be supplied which would enable us to see the connections, if we are to make any sense of what they say and do.

Now, it seems to me that this provides us with a way of rejecting the assumption which underlies the theories of Hare and Mrs. Foot. For, if what I have said is true, we can at once admit that there are rules governing what can count as a moral reason, and deny that there is anything common to all moral reasons. For on my account the rules are of a quite different kind altogether. Instead of asserting that if something is a moral reason it must possess some elusive property in common with all other moral reasons, they tell us that it can only be accepted as a moral reason if it stands in some relation to the other things that we accept as moral reasons. We see, then, that while Hare is right to say that criteria of goodness are not always determined, he is wrong to say that they are ever a matter of personal decision.

[1] I do not think that in these circumstances we could say with any conviction that moral considerations *were* involved. If someone were to maintain that this were so, then I should want to know what made them think that the issues in question were moral and not (say) legal ones.

4

The Diversity of Moral Standards

What I tried to do in the last chapter was to outline an account of moral reasoning which would avoid some of the errors detected in the writings of Hare and Mrs. Foot. But, I have as yet only sketched the outlines of a moral theory. It must now be expanded in greater detail. And the way in which I intend to do this is by considering some of the main objections to which it might appear to be vulnerable.

I want to begin with two objections which, although they raise what are to some extent different issues, may for the purposes of this essay be regarded as two species of the same objection.

1. The first of these draws attention to the enormous diversity in the ideas of morality held by people in different communities. To deny the existence of cultures whose members justify their beliefs and actions in ways quite different from our own, would be to fly in the face of historical and anthropological fact. Palamades, a character in one of Hume's dialogues, emphasises the importance for moral philosophy of recognising such differences:

> The Athenians, surely, were a civilised, intelligent people, if ever there were one; and yet their man of merit might, in this age, be held in horror and execration. The French are also, without doubt, a very civilised, intelligent people; and yet their man of merit might, with the Athenians, be an object of the highest contempt and ridicule, and even hatred. And what renders the matter more extraordinary: these two people are supposed to be the most similar in

their national character of any in ancient and modern times. . . .
What wide differences, therefore, in the sentiments of morals must
be found between civilised nations and barbarians.[1]

Now, differences like those to which Palamades draws attention might seem to present difficulties for my account. Let me explain this. The crux of what I said in the last chapter was that something would count as a moral reason only if it bore some relation to considerations already accepted as such. In this way I tried to show that a moral reason cannot be *anything* which the individual chooses to mention. But against this someone might want to argue that although within any way of life (e.g. that of a Christian or that of a Buddhist monk) we may be able to draw limits to what can be counted as morally relevant, no such limits will apply to any conceivable morality.

Palamades, in the above dialogue, amasses a great deal of evidence to show that many of the characteristics regarded by the Athenians as virtues would be regarded in his time as grounds for condemning a man. Even if, as Hume objects, he tends to exaggerate his points, it is undeniable that such differences exist. And, if so, is it not conceivable that the type of justification given in our morality may be wholly different from that given in another? Surely, so the objection runs, we can at least imagine that there should be, or have been, civilisations where what we call virtues are regarded as vices, or where the same importance which we attach to concepts like murder and adultery is given to considerations to which we should attach no importance whatsoever. How then can there be any limits to what counts as a moral reason?

2. The second type of argument rests its case on the fact that there are certain types of moral position which we regard as being in some way revolutionary. The case of the revolutionary (the radical, the anarchist) seems to present even greater conceptual difficulties for my theory than does the existence of alien ways of life. For in this essay I wish to

[1] 'A Dialogue', p. 296.

The Diversity of Moral Standards

emphasise the importance of accepted standards and tradition in morality. To this the obvious diversity of moral standards does *prima facie* present an objection. But because people belong to different ages or different parts of the world it does not necessarily follow, although it is perhaps likely, that they will hold views different from our own. We can imagine what it would be like for all men always to agree on matters of morals, even though we may want to say that such a state of affairs is improbable. The revolutionary, on the other hand, would not be the sort of person that he is, unless he rejected the accepted moral standards of his time. Chekhov is making this sort of point when he says:

> If you cry 'Forward', you must without fail make plain in what direction to go. Don't you see that if, without doing so, you call out the word to both a monk and a revolutionary, they will go in directions precisely opposite.

The monk regards progress as something based on an adherence to certain norms. The revolutionary sees it as consisting in a rejection of these norms. Does it not distort the picture, it might be argued, to insist that the views of the monk and those of the revolutionary must necessarily be related in some way if they are both to count as moral views?

Let us consider each of these arguments in turn and see whether either constitutes any objection to the thesis which I am maintaining.

The first objection was that my account ignores the diversity of moral codes. And even if, as I shall try to show, the criticism is unjustified here, it is undoubtedly a powerful objection to many other moral theories, and in particular to one of the two theories with which this essay is concerned. For it does not seem to me that Mrs. Foot's account can give any convincing explanation of the sort of differences which Palamades emphasises. As we have seen, it is her intention in her later articles[1] to assimilate moral judgements like 'That was a despicable thing to do' to empirical statements like 'There is a cabbage in the next room'. I should not be said to know the meaning of the word 'cabbage' unless I knew that it is evidence against something being a cabbage that it has a bright yellow skin which peels easily. Mrs. Foot wishes to say that the same is true of moral terms. She contends that just as the evidence for saying that something is a cabbage is laid down by the meaning of the word, so the evidence for saying that some action is despicable is laid down by the meaning of the word 'despicable'. The consequences of this are clear. We cannot conceive of an ultimate disagreement between people of different cultures about whether or not some vegetable counts as a cabbage. Nor, on Mrs. Foot's account, can we conceive of an ultimate disagreement between people of different cultures over whether some action is despicable or not. Whether this is at all plausible we shall have to consider later. But in any case it remains true to say that Mrs. Foot is unable to account for the possibility of an alien moral code. If it turned out that there could be ultimate moral disagreements (moral breakdowns), then Mrs. Foot would have to insist that one party to the dispute was not holding a moral position.

It is to Hare's credit that, unlike Mrs. Foot and a great many other theorists, he does not attempt to camouflage the differences between moral codes. He rightly rejects any search for 'a method of argument which would force people to the same conclusion whatever the world and the people in it were like'.[2] But, as we have seen, he can do this only because he does not recognise any limit to what can count as a morality. If we refuse to call such borderline cases as the code which the Sicilian Mafiosi or the Nazis espoused moralities, then this is a purely terminological question, and 'nothing in morals . . . turns on the actual use of words'.[3] In

[1] And it should be noted that my remarks apply *only* to her later articles. They do not apply to the remarks in 'When is a Principle a Moral Principle?' with which I largely agree.

[2] *Freedom and Reason*, p. 184.   [3] Ibid., p. 164.

The Diversity of Moral Standards

consequence, Hare is unable to explain why we regard such cases as in some way borderline, or why it might take argument to make us agree that they were moralities. If it is open to us to choose what we shall call a morality, then there is nothing to explain.

Now, if I am to reject both of these views, two things require explanation. On the one hand we must show that different ways of life can still be regarded as moralities, even if there are irreducible differences between them, which is what Mrs. Foot denies. And on the other, we have to show that it is nevertheless possible to draw limits to what can be counted as a moral consideration, regardless of the way of life in which it occurs, which is what Hare denies.

I shall begin by considering two situations where it is clear that a moral justification for an action is being given. The first is to be found in A. I. Kuprin's *The Duel*. In this story a second-lieutenant, Romashov, has been ordered by his superiors to fight a duel with a man whom he has insulted. On learning of this, his friend Nazansky is horrified, and asks:

> 'But why, Romashov, for whatever reason should you go through with such an imbecility? You know that you have the courage to fight – it would take more courage to refuse.' 'But he hit me first . . . ,' Romashov said stubbornly, and a wave of anger stirred painfully in his chest.
>
> 'All right, so he hit you,' Nazansky said patiently and sadly. 'But does it matter so much? You'll forget the offence and the hatred it aroused in you soon enough, but it would take much longer to forget a man you'd killed. Idiots, brass-hats, and multi-coloured parrots have discovered a difference between murder in a duel and just plain murder. But the important thing about a murder is not the style it's done in, nor the courage or cowardice displayed.... The one significant fact is that life is withdrawn from a human being.'[1]

The second situation is that faced by Jeannie Deans in Scott's *The Heart of Midlothian*. Jeannie's sister, Effie, has concealed the birth of her dead child. Under the Scottish penal

---

[1] *The Duel*, pp. 179–80.

Moral Reasoning

laws she is presumed guilty of murder and will suffer the death penalty unless Jeannie swears that she was told of her sister's pregnancy. She discusses the matter with Effie's lover and the father of the child, George Robertson, who tries to persuade her to perjure herself:

> 'You will remember all this – that is all that is necessary to be said.'
> 'But I cannot remember,' answered Jeannie with simplicity, 'that which Effie never told me.'
> 'Are you so dull – so very dull of apprehension,' he exclaimed, 'you must repeat this tale . . . before these justices – justiciary – whatever they call their bloodthirsty court, and save your sister from being murdered.'
> 'I wad ware the best blood in my body to keep her skaithless,' said Jeannie, weeping in bitter agony, 'but I cannot change right into wrong, nor make true that which is false.'[1]

Now what I am here concerned with is the role of concepts like murder and truth-telling in arguments such as these. For it seems to me that they have a fundamental part to play in enabling us to recognise something as a moral belief, or as a moral justification. I want to begin by making two comments about this role.

The first thing to be noticed is that when Nazansky defends his criticism of duelling by pointing out that killing a man in a duel is still murder, we recognise that here no further defence can be given. Again, when Jeannie Deans refuses to do George Robertson's bidding by telling a lie, we recognise that her conviction that lying is wrong is a complete justification for her decision. In both cases it would be pointless to ask for further reasons, for none could be given. Now I suggest that the same is true of many other moral concepts. When an action is defended or condemned by characterising it as integrity, greed, adultery, suicide, and so on, we are usually forced to conclude that an ultimate justification has been offered. True, in *one* sense it may still be possible for someone to request and be given further

---

[1] *The Heart of Midlothian*, p. 163.

reasons. For example, if I condemn something as an act of adultery, it may be possible for someone to ask me, 'Why is that a reason?', and for me to answer, perhaps by drawing attention to the importance which is attached to the institution of marriage in my society and the conventions which surround it. But here the conversation has moved on to a somewhat different level. I am no longer justifying my condemnation of a particular action, but rather explaining what is involved in adultery. (In the same way, if we ask a friend why he is looking for a drinking-fountain, and he answers, 'I'm thirsty', it will not make sense to ask for a further reason. We might still ask 'Why?', but here the question will be of a different kind. The sort of answer which we now expect is, for example, 'I've been eating salty food', or 'It's the sun'. Neither of these explains why being thirsty is grounds for seeking a drinking-fountain, but rather why our friend is thirsty in the first place.) Concepts like honesty, murder, integrity bring the chain of reasons given in an argument to an end.

Concepts like honesty, murder, integrity also enable us to see the reasons given in an argument as moral reasons. We see this most clearly in *The Duel*. Romashov can see his duel with Nikolaev only as a means of satisfying his craving for the respect of his fellow-officers. Nazansky *could* have replied by pointing to the possibility that Romashov would himself be killed. This would have been another consideration to be weighed alongside the possibility of his attaining his desired end. Romashov might even have ignored it completely. But when Nazansky introduces the consideration of murder, the whole character of the conversation changes. It is placed in a moral context. Romashov realises this. He recognises that Nazansky is introducing moral issues which *cannot* merely be ignored because of personal preference. Again, while we could not recognise a reference to the possibility of Romashov being killed as a moral reason for his declining to fight, if it were merely an appeal to his own self-interest, we might well do so if we think of someone for whom this would count as suicide. For suicide is another concept which establishes that a context is a moral one, whereas self-interest is not.

Now what these two points seem to show is that there is a range of concepts (murder, adultery, suicide, truth-telling, etc.) which are in some sense constitutive of a morality. For, in the first place, it is they which enable us to recognise a justification as a moral justification, and in the second they do so conclusively, for they indicate a person's whole moral outlook. When we have difficulty in deciding whether some way of life is a morality, it is the presence or absence of such concepts which decides the question, although, as I have mentioned,[1] there will be cases where no such decision is possible, where we simply cannot say whether a people possesses a morality or not. It is also the presence or absence of such concepts which decides what type of morality it is. The Christian morality places a premium on such virtues as humility, self-sacrifice, charity, whereas a military ethic will emphasise the importance of courage, strength, integrity, and so on.

This shows why ways of life which differ so greatly from our own may nevertheless be regarded as moralities. For despite the differences there will also be similarities. Recognising these similarities is not just a matter of drawing analogies between the particular reasons given in these cultures. Rather it is a matter of seeing the connections between their central concepts and our own. For it is these central concepts, like murder for instance, which establish finally how other people see the actions they perform, the judgements which they make, and the particular reasons which they give.

Hume, in the article mentioned earlier, makes a similar point against Palamades. Palamades, as we have seen, can only see the immense differences between the moral beliefs of the Athenians and those of his own time. But Hume emphasises the similarities – similarities which are to be recognised by

[1] Chapter 3, pp. 35–6

examining the first principles, which each nation establishes, of blame and censure. The Rhine flows north, the Rhone south; but both spring from the same mountain. . . . In how many circumstances would an Athenian and a Frenchman of merit certainly resemble one another? Good sense, knowledge, wit, eloquence, humanity, fidelity, truth, justice, courage, temperance, constancy, dignity of mind; these you have all omitted.[1]

It is primarily because of the presence of these concepts that we regard the Athenian way of life as a morality. For it is through them that it has points of contact with other moralities.

It is important to note that my own theory is not intended as a decision in favour of any particular morality. This, I believe, would be an error, for it is not the task of the moral philosopher to persuade others to adopt his own moral viewpoint or to give moral advice, if indeed this task belongs to anyone. Probably the vast majority of present-day people would agree with Nazansky in condemning duelling. But it does not follow that we cannot take seriously a society in which it is regarded as wholly commendable. For this could well be a moral belief. We see how this might be so if we imagine a race who see it as the mark of a courageous man that he is willing to risk his life in this way, or that he has such a high regard for the honour of his wife and friends that he is willing to take up the sword against those who do not respect it. Here the reference to considerations like courage and respect establishes the context as a moral one. On the other hand, if there were a complete divorce between the beliefs of some society and those of our own, it would be impossible for us to understand any of these beliefs in the same way that we understand the different attitudes towards duelling, that is as moral attitudes. Certainly we might nevertheless be disinclined to say that they did *not* possess a morality. One does not reject a people's beliefs simply on the ground that one does not understand them, for it may be that there is a connection between their beliefs and ours which we have not yet noticed. My point is simply that

[1] Hume, op. cit., p. 297.

unless such connections could be found, then we should have no sufficient reason for saying with any conviction that they possessed a morality. The question would remain open.

Unfortunately, in chapter 9 of *The Language of Morals*, Hare produces what might seem to be a decisive counter-example to my remarks, for he seems to have succeeded in describing a situation which, if what I have said is true, ought to be indescribable; namely something which could be recognised as a morality, even though it undoubtedly has no points of contact with our own. He invites us to imagine the following situation:

> A missionary armed with a grammar-book lands on a desert island. The vocabulary of his grammar-book gives him the equivalent in the cannibal's language of the English word 'good', . . . If the missionary has mastered his vocabulary, he can. . . . communicate with them (the cannibals)[1] about morals quite happily. They know that when he uses the word, he is commending the person or object that he applies it to. The only thing they will find odd is that he applies it to such strange people, people who are meek and gentle and do not collect large quantities of scalps. . . . But they and the missionary are under no misapprehension about the meaning, in the evaluative sense, of the word 'good'; it is the word one uses for commending. If they were under such a misapprehension, moral communication between them would be impossible. . . . Even if the qualities in people which the missionary commended had nothing in common with the qualities which the cannibals commended, yet they would both know what the word 'good' meant.[2]

Now it might well seem that we can easily imagine the sort of situation described above, and that my arguments in this section are therefore necessarily misleading. But I think that this would be a mistake. For what is to be noticed is that in this passage Hare covertly begs all the most important questions. He assumes, e.g. that 'good' (English) and 'good' (cannibal) are equivalent and that the missionary could know this. But, we want to ask, how could he, if the situation is really as Hare describes it? Nor does it answer

[1] My comment.   [2] *The Language of Morals*, p. 148.

The Diversity of Moral Standards

the question to say that the missionary learns his vocabulary from a grammar-book. For we now have to enquire how the men who compiled this grammar-book could have discovered the alleged equivalence between 'good' (English) and 'good' (cannibal), unless they had been able to observe certain similarities between the qualities to which the cannibals applied it, and those to which they themselves applied it. My answer is that they could not have done so. Further, I should want to say that if the personal qualities which the cannibals commended had absolutely nothing in common with those which the missionary commended, he would soon begin to wonder whether his grammar-book was not misleading him in some way.

Again Hare tells us that the missionary and the cannibals will 'be able to communicate about morals quite happily',[1] and he appears to think that this would be true even if there were no points of contact between their respective beliefs. But this suggestion has a superficial plausibility only because Hare never considers what such a complete divorce of beliefs would be like. True the people whom he describes follow a way of life which the missionary would probably find repugnant. They are cannibals, he tells us, and they tend to approve of men who are 'bold and burly and collect more scalps than the average'.[2] But it would surely be quite wrong to suppose that such views could have no connection with the Christian morality of the missionary. At the very least they have this in common that they attach some importance to the virtue of courage. Again, Hare does not tell us what he means by cannibalism, and if this signifies *merely* the taste for human flesh, then it is difficult to see this as a moral convention (and I do not think that anyone would think that it was, even the cannibals). But generally cannibalism is itself connected with moral beliefs. It may, for instance, be a mark of respect for a great warrior killed in battle. In *The Golden Bough* Frazer remarks that:

> The Nauras Indians of New Grenada ate the hearts of the

[1] Hare, op. cit.   [2] Ibid.

Spaniards when they had the opportunity, hoping thereby to make themselves as dauntless as the dreaded Castilian chivalry.[1]

The notion of respect for the dead is not a difficult one for a Christian missionary to understand,[2] and we can imagine that even with such tenuous points of contact between missionary and cannibals there should be some discussion between them. But suppose that the cannibal use of the term 'good' were governed by such factors as the length of a man's fingernails or the colour of his eyes. I cannot see that if this were the case the missionary would find much common ground for discussion. Indeed I fail to see how he could even begin to understand such beliefs. Hare is willing to admit only that such uses of the word 'good' would be unusual. In his paper to the British Academy, 'Descriptivism', he says:

> If a man said that a man was a good man because he clasped and unclasped his hands, we should indeed at first find ourselves wondering whether we had understood him. But the reason is that although what he says is perfectly comprehensible in its literal sense, it is very odd indeed for anyone to think it.[3]

But surely this only confuses the distinction between unusual moral conventions and those which are unintelligible, between 'That is not what we normally do' and 'That is unintelligible'. Cannibalism is, in the present age, unusual; yet it is, as I have tried to show, intelligible as a moral convention. But, as it stands, and without further explanation, respecting a man for clasping his hands is unintelligible. When Hare denies this, it is difficult to see

---

[1] *The Golden Bough*, p. 497.
[2] I am not suggesting that there is only one reason why a race might regard cannibalism as having moral significance. This would, I think, be a mistake, although one which Frazer himself tends to make. Clearly the convention of cannibalism (like in our own society the convention of capital punishment) may have been supported by different peoples for different reasons. The point which I wish to make is simply that it is at least conceivable that these should be *moral* reasons.
[3] 'Descriptivism', p. 130.

The Diversity of Moral Standards

what he *would* count as an unintelligible belief, or how he could distinguish between sense and nonsense here.

Before we leave this topic, however, it might be worthwhile to consider one possible defence which might be made of Hare's account.

I have been arguing that we regard an alien way of life as a morality only where the reasons that its participants give bear certain resemblances to what other people regard as moral reasons. But it might be thought that even where this is not so, their life may resemble ours in *other* ways, sufficiently to justify us in saying that they definitely possess a morality. This would seem to be the sort of argument advanced by J. Harrison in the symposium 'When is a Principle a Moral Principle?' In reply to certain criticisms of Hare by Mrs. Foot, Harrison asserts that:

> Though I may be (linguistically) eccentric, I personally would say that a man who exhibited signs of remorse when he stepped on the black lines of a pavement, tried to persuade others not to step on them, tried to make unlined pavements by law compulsory, and so on, did hold this as a moral principle. It is true that I should also say that he was very probably mad, but why should not insanity manifest itself in moral as well as factual delusions? And though we may think his moral views erroneous, is he otherwise so very different, logically or psychologically, from ourselves? I have little doubt that his moral promptings are just like ours – which suggests that morality may be no more than a socially useful compulsive neurosis – and no doubt at all that he can give as good reasons for his moral views as we can give for ours, i.e. none at all.[1]

Now, like Hare, Harrison clearly thinks that anything whatsoever (even stepping on the lines of a pavement) could play the same part in the life of a community as, for example, murder does in ours. Harrison admits that in such a community, the reasons men give for their actions and beliefs could have no connections with those which we give. So on my account there would be no sufficient justification for saying that they possess a morality (although we may be disinclined to deny that this is so). But it is clear from the

[1] 'When is a Principle a Moral Principle?', p. 113.

last sentence in the above passage that Harrison does not regard reasons as playing any important part in morality. There may be other and, he feels, more important resemblances between our own life and that of others. And if we ask, 'What resemblances could there be between people of two such different cultures as these?', then I think that his answer would be that they might resemble us in that (for example) they also show signs of remorse, or act in a guilty manner when they do certain things, or that they become indignant when they see other people doing these things. Indeed the introduction of concepts like 'guilt' and 'remorse' may well seem to clinch the matter. For surely one can feel remorse for anything, and isn't the fact that someone feels remorse for what he has done, grounds for saying that he regards it as morally wrong? It seems to follow that if members of another society show signs of guilt or pangs of remorse whenever they tread on the lines of a pavement, we shall be forced to conclude that they regard this as morally evil, for it seems to play the same part in their lives as do such accepted evils as adultery in ours.

What then is wrong with this sort of argument? The fundamental mistake seems to lie in the assumption that terms like 'remorse' and 'guilt' refer only to a pattern of behaviour. On Harrison's view of the matter, it is just a brute fact that men exhibit this behaviour only when they are responsible for things like murder and adultery. It might result from any action whatsoever. So there is no real reason why they should not feel remorse for anything one cared to mention. If there are limits they are psychological and not conceptual.

I submit that this argument is just a confusion. It is a mistake to suppose that a man can (logically) feel remorse for anything whatsoever. For the significant point is that to say that a man feels or shows remorse is *already* to assume that he has done something which *can* be regarded as morally reprehensible. No doubt one can only be said to feel remorse if one acts in a certain way. We do not say that young Johnny feels remorse for hitting his baby brother, if

The Diversity of Moral Standards

he continues to victimise the child as soon as its mother's back is turned. But it does not follow that to say of someone that he feels remorse is simply to say that his behaviour exhibits certain characteristics. For if this were so, then there would be no objection to saying that he felt remorse even where he himself admitted that he had done nothing which he regarded as wrong. Rather it is to interpret his behaviour by linking it to something evil which he has done. However much a man might hang his head or apologise, whenever he stepped on the lines of a pavement, we should be disinclined to say that he felt remorse unless he were able to explain how this action could be regarded as immoral, although we might well say that he was feigning remorse, or perhaps, as Harrison says, that he was mad. Certainly, given that a man does seem to act in this way, we shall do well to look carefully at his way of life in order to see whether the lines on the pavement do not have a special significance for him, which we have missed. Probably we shall come to the conclusion that they do. All that I am denying is that by itself his behaviour could give sufficient grounds for such a conclusion.

One possible objection to this would be that we *do* sometimes use such terms in ways which seem to offer some support for Harrison's way of speaking. In particular it might be thought that their application to the behaviour of animals and small children is a case in point. Thus, for example, I might say that my pet spaniel looks guilty, if he hides in a corner and refuses his food after chewing my slippers. And here the conditions of the term's use seem to be purely behavioural. Given suitable training, there is no reason to suppose that an animal might not come to exhibit the same sort of reaction for breaches of any rule we chose to invent, however absurd. We should still say that what he felt was guilt. What must be noted here is that when we say that an animal feels remorse or shows guilt, this is an anthropomorphic way of speaking. We see this if we compare it with the use of terms like 'fear' or 'anger' to refer to animal behaviour. Suppose that I go to strike my spaniel, and he rolls his eyes and flinches. We should say that he is afraid. And we should say this partly because we know that spaniels do not like being struck. Our saying that he shows fear reflects the interests of the dog and not of human beings. For we could explain what is involved in an animal being afraid without any reference to human activities. On the other hand, when I say that my spaniel feels guilty for having chewed my slippers, what I say reflects my interests and beliefs, and not those of the animal. It is I who have to have slippers repaired, and so regard their destruction as wrong. (It would, in any case, be absurd to attribute any moral belief to an animal.) And it is only in relation to this belief of mine that it makes sense to suppose that what the dog feels is remorse or guilt.

Harrison's argument then rests on a confusion. And it is a confusion which has been increased rather than lessened by the attempts of contemporary psychologists to investigate the nature of morality. An example is Eysenck's *Fact and Fiction in Psychology*. In a chapter called 'Crime, Conscience and Conditioning', Eysenck describes an experiment[1] carried out by one R. L. Solomon in which six-month-old puppies were offered a choice between horsemeat and a commercial dog-food. When the puppies chose the former they were hit with a rolled-up newspaper, and in this way conditioned to avoid horsemeat. The puppies were then starved for forty-eight hours and offered a dish of this foodstuff. Eysenck observes that those which took the horsemeat displayed certain emotional disturbances, which he refers to as 'guilt-reactions'.

Now, if all that Eysenck wishes to do here is to introduce a mnemonic term which will enable him to refer to a certain pattern of behaviour, then this may be justifiable (although it is by no means clear why such a term is needed, since what the puppies exhibited was simply fear of being swatted with a newspaper). But it is clear that this is not all that he wishes to do. For he regards Solomon's experiment as evidence for the claim that 'conscience is simply a conditioned reflex',

[1] *Fact and Fiction in Psychology*, pp. 262–4.

and concludes that human morality is just the effect of social conditioning. And this is plausible only if 'guilt' is here being used in its normal sense. But, as we have seen, the puppies' behaviour could constitute guilt in this sense only if it were excited by something recognised as morally evil. Eysenck himself implicitly recognises this, and in order to make his argument at all plausible, he presupposes that 'in this situation eating the horsemeat is the immoral activity which is to be eliminated'. There is, of course, no ground for supposing that eating horsemeat could be in any way immoral. In the sense in which Eysenck is using the word 'guilt', the puppies' guilt is not a moral phenomenon at all, and can therefore throw no light on the way in which humans acquire their moral beliefs.

It would seem then that Eysenck makes just the same sort of mistake as Harrison. Both try to apply words like 'guilt' and 'remorse' on purely behavioural grounds, and then use the existence of such behaviour as a criterion for saying that someone (or something) possesses a moral belief. And this is a fallacious argument. For whether these terms are used of human behaviour, or anthropomorphically of animal behaviour, they presuppose the existence of moral beliefs. They cannot be used as the criterion of the existence of a morality.

5
The Rebel and Moral Traditions

Let us now turn our attention to the second objection to my account, that is, the claim that it gives a distorted picture of the nature of revolutionary ideas in morality.

The rebel, I remarked, *is* a rebel just in so far as he rejects the accepted scale of values of his society. This is what it means to be a rebel. So we might be inclined to say that there can be no point of contact between the views which he expresses and those expressed by 'society'. If this *is* so, and if we are to accept the theory which I have proposed in this essay, we seem to be presented with a dilemma. For we appear to be forced to one of two conclusions: (*a*) that the views of a rebel like Nietzsche, Kierkegaard, Marx, Tolstoi, or Christ are literally unintelligible, despite our strong feeling that what they say is new and important, or (*b*) that, although intelligible, their views belong to some sphere other than that of morality.

My answer to this objection is to deny the premiss upon which it is founded. I do not believe that it is necessary to adopt either of these alternatives, simply because I do not think that it is true to say that the views of the revolutionary have no points of contact with other moralities, nor even that they have no points of contact with the moral position that he is rejecting. Of course, this is not to deny that the rebel may reject a great many of our moral beliefs, perhaps even the majority of them. What I *do* maintain is that he cannot be understood in complete independence of *all*

The Rebel and Moral Traditions

accepted moral beliefs. What he says is intelligible only because it can be seen to have connections with a tradition which encompasses both what he accepts and what he rejects.

Let us begin by considering the views of Friedrich Nietzsche. I choose Nietzsche because he, of all revolutionaries in the field of morals, seems to have least in common with traditional morality. Certainly a cursory reading of a work like *Beyond Good and Evil* leaves one with the impression that Nietzsche rejects everything of importance in any morality. Piety, we are told, is no more than a technique by which a man 'can become so artful, so superficial, so iridescent, and so good, that his appearance no longer offends',[1] he questions the value of truth and suggests that perhaps 'a higher and more fundamental value for life should be ascribed to the will, to delusion, to selfishness, and cupidity'.[2] Humility occupies a central place among the Christian virtues, but Nietzsche condemns 'the ideal of a silly, renouncing, humble, selfless, humanity',[3] and submits that 'egoism belongs to the essence of a noble soul'.[4] Indeed, often he seems to regard goodness as itself suspect, and this may give the impression that his ideal is one of evil.

Despite this, I do not think that it is true to say that Nietzsche's views, as expressed in *Beyond Good and Evil*, have nothing in common with traditional morality. And I want to try to show that it is possible for him to criticise many of the traditional moral values as he does, only because there are others which he does not question.

It is a truism to say that a man's ideas are intelligible only within a certain context, and that to understand them we require some understanding of the way of life and traditions to which they belong. To this the rebel is no exception. As Simone Weil says:

> Like all human activities, the revolution draws all its vigour from a tradition.[5]

[1] *Beyond Good and Evil*, p. 79.   [2] Ibid., p. 7.
[3] Ibid., p. 154.   [4] Ibid., p. 240.   [5] *The Need for Roots*, p. 49.

But this is also true of the ideas of the rebel in a special sense. For, as I have said, what makes a man a rebel are his criticisms of the accepted views. And this means that in order to assess the value of his contributions, we need some understanding of the way of life which he is attacking.

Now, in the case of Nietzsche, this presents difficulties. Not, of course, because there is any doubt about *what* he wished to criticise. True, he characterised the subject of his attacks in many different ways: as 'herding-animal morality', as 'slave-morality', as 'gregarious European morality', and sometimes just as 'morality'. But it is not hard to see what sort of thing he wanted to denounce. Like Kierkegaard (in *The Present Age*, for instance), Nietzsche felt that European morality had become a matter of mere convention, unreflective, without passion or enthusiasm, and indeed without strong feelings of any kind. It was, in fact, a morality for the weak man, particularly the weak-willed man.

> According to the servile mode of thought, the good man must in any case be the *safe* man; he is good-natured, easily deceived, perhaps a little stupid, *un bonhomme*.[1]

Under the influence of people like the utilitarians, the virtues had degenerated into mere recipes for avoiding danger and for preserving a superficial degree of comfort in the state. Moreover, in a morality of fear, such as Nietzsche regarded European morality, it was not unnatural that the powerful man, the man of imagination, the exceptional man should be regarded as evil, for it is he who provides the greatest danger to the accepted way of life. And it was against this that Nietzsche rebelled. He had no time for a culture whose ideal it was to turn man into 'a pygmy with equal rights and claims'.[2]

The difficulties in Nietzsche's work which I mentioned earlier occur not when we try to say *what* he was attacking but when we try to say *how* he wished to criticise it. I want now to consider two possible answers to this question, in order to show that what Nietzsche says can be understood

---

[1] Nietzsche, op. cit., p. 231. [2] Ibid., p. 131.

only because of its dependence on certain traditional moral concepts.

1. One way in which we can regard Nietzsche's work is as an attack not upon genuine morality, but upon some sort of perversion of morality. Sometimes he talks as if the beliefs he is attacking are not moral beliefs at all (even though they are expressed in moral terms) but pseudo-moral beliefs. Consider, for instance, his criticism of the slave-virtues of humility and honesty. When Nietzsche talks of 'refined, artful humility',[1] he is referring not to true humility, but rather to a perversion of it, a perversion which is well illustrated in a passage from Dickens' *David Copperfield*.

> Father and me was both brought up in a foundation-school for boys. ... They taught us all a deal of umbleness – not much else that I know of from morning to night. We was to be umble to this person and umble to that; and to pull off our caps here and to make bows there; and always to know our places and to abase ourselves before our betters. Father got the monitor-medal by being umble. So did I. Father got made a sexton by being umble. He had the character among the gentle-folks of being such a well-behaved man, that they were determined to bring him in. 'Be umble,' says father to me, 'and you'll get on. It was always being dinned into you and me at school; it's what goes down best. Be umble,' says father, 'and you'll do,' And really it ain't done bad. I got to know what umbleness did, and I took to it. I ate umble pie with an appetite.[2]

Uriah Heep's 'humility' (like the 'humility' of the slave-moralist) is not a virtue, but only what Adeimantus in Plato's *Republic* refers to as 'an imposing façade designed to look like virtue'.[3] True humility, the humility of the saint, *is* a virtue. The difference between the two becomes clear when we ask why it is that Uriah Heep attaches such importance to acting in a humble manner. I think that it is obvious that for him 'humility' is a means for attaining certain ends, a way to 'get on'. Uriah Heep *uses* humility in order to disguise his true motives, which are disreputable ones, and

---

[1] Nietzsche, op. cit. p. 188.   [2] *David Copperfield*, p. 480.
[3] *Republic*, 365 c, p. 49.

to gain the respect of others. Unlike the truly virtuous person, for whom humility is important in itself, and who can offer no reason for so regarding it, Uriah Heep attaches no importance to humility in itself. Rather it is his ends which are important to him. It just so happens that 'humility' is a way of attaining these ends. This becomes clear towards the end of the book. When Heep feels that this humility can no longer help him, he rejects it. As David Copperfield observes:

> Though I had long known that his servility was false, and all his pretence knavish and hollow, I had no adequate conception of the extent of his hypocrisy, until I saw him with his mask off. The suddenness with which he dropped it, when he perceived that it was useless to him; the malice, insolence, and hatred he revealed ... at first took even me by surprise, who had known him so long and disliked him so heartily.[1]

Similar considerations apply to Nietzsche's remarks about 'frankness' and 'honesty' on p. 200 of *Beyond Good and Evil*. The Germans, he tells us, love frankness and honesty:

> It is so *convenient* to be frank and honest. – This confidingness, this complaisance, this showing-the-cards of German honesty, is probably the most dangerous and most successful disguise which the German is up to nowadays. ... It is wise for a people to pose and let itself be regarded as profound, clumsy, good-natured, honest and foolish.

What Nietzsche seems to have in mind here is the sort of thing which is often referred to as 'speaking one's mind' or 'bluntness'. Unlike pseudo-humility, this need not be in any way evil. We may well have respect for a person's integrity, even though we may want to say that the world would be a happier place if they did not make such a fetish of honesty. On the other hand, there are people whose outspokenness is only a front. What the gossip says, ostensibly from a desire to tell the truth, may in fact stem from a desire to hurt others. The man who prides himself on his uprightness and frankness may well only be seeking the admiration

---

[1] Dickens, op. cit., p. 504.

of others; and we are all familiar with the sort of person who, having failed to get his way by means of deception and trickery, decides to 'put all his cards on the table'. For him, honesty has a value only as a technique for attaining his ends.

In drawing attention to this sort of hypocrisy, in showing how it is possible for men to deceive themselves and others, Nietzsche was saying something important and interesting. But I think that it is essential to be quite clear about the way in which this sort of criticism is to be understood. For while it makes sense construed as an attack on particular *uses* of morality, various ailments to which morality is prone, it is just a confusion to suppose that it might be the basis of an attack on morality in general. To say that much of what we call humility is merely hypocrisy, is no criticism of true humility.

Unfortunately, Mrs. Foot, in a recent article on Nietzsche, tends to ignore this point. And this leads her to misinterpret the nature of his views. She believes that it is wrong to suppose that Nietzsche wished to criticise only a particular approach to morality, 'for did he not declare war, not only on the "slave-morality" of Christianity, but on morality itself?'[1] One of Mrs. Foot's reasons for saying this appears at the end of the article. Nietzsche, she tells us, felt that

> morality does not even make a man moral, and so must be condemned by its own standards. No one has described better than he the self-interest and malice, as well as the weaknesses, that can lie behind a kindly concern for others.[2]

Now, so far I have been trying to show that Nietzsche was concerned in his writings to bring to light and criticise various kinds of hypocrisy. His remarks about humility are an attack on one form which this evil can take, and as such they are valuable, for this is an evil to which all moral codes are liable.

However, it is a quite different thing to maintain that morality is *just* hypocrisy, and this is what Nietzsche's

'Immoralist', p. 10.   [2] Ibid.

criticisms amount to if they are construed as an attack, not on a particular perversion of morality, but on morality itself. The point is that hypocrisy is parasitic on true virtue. We see this in the case of Uriah Heep. Heep is able to give his actions a cloak of respectability by disguising them as humility. But he is able to do so only because those with whom he has dealings do genuinely regard humility as a virtue. Just as the orators who Socrates attacked in the *Gorgias* traded on the fact that 'lecturing and oratory are apt to be confused in the popular mind as occupying common ground',[1] so Uriah Heep trades on the fact that humility and pseudo-humility can be confused. But it is essential to this sort of deception that there should be people capable of being taken in by it (like Dickens' Mr. Wickfield, who professes to 'one plain motive' in all that he does, and 'looks for single motives in everyone'), that is to say, people who are not hypocrites and who regard humility as something to be valued in itself. The sorts of double-mindedness which Nietzsche and Dickens describe are necessarily the exception, for they can occur only in a community where there is a genuine regard for virtue. The former's criticisms of slave-morality do not make sense if we regard them as an attack on morality itself.

Now, in so far as Nietzsche's attacks on slave-morality are merely an attack on various types of hypocrisy, then it is not difficult to see that his position is a moral one. For deception is involved in the very nature of hypocrisy. The hypocrite is essentially someone who aims at deceiving others about his motives. And Nietzsche's criticisms of slave-morality can be understood as moral criticisms because of the appeal to considerations like 'sincerity' and 'integrity' which they involve.

2. On the other hand, Nietzsche often seems to talk as if slave-morality were indeed a genuine morality (and not just a technique for deceiving others), but a morality which *he* rejects in favour of another. This type of approach is suggested towards the end of chapter 5, where he is attacking

[1] *Gorgias*, 466 c, p. 47.

The Rebel and Moral Traditions

the idea that the virtues of 'the gregarious European man', 'public spirit, kindness, deference, industry, temperance, modesty . . . are the peculiarly human virtues'.[1] Nietzsche objects that European morality is

> only one kind of human morality, beside which, before which, and after which many other moralities, and above all *higher* moralities, are or should be possible.[2]

But even if the morality which Nietzsche is attacking is a genuine morality, there are no grounds for supposing that what he advocates must be something other than morality, or that his views are therefore unintelligible. True he rejects concepts which are central to many moral codes, but he does so because he thinks that, in emphasising these, traditional morality has tended to ignore other things which he regards as more important, virtues like courage, strength of character, sensitivity, passion,[3] and it is concepts like these which enable us to see his views as moral views. Furthermore, when we see that it is concepts like these which are central to the Nietzschean ethic, it then becomes easier to understand some of the things which he says, which we might be inclined to think could not express a moral attitude. He says, for example:

> You want if possible (and there is no more insane 'if possible') to *do away with suffering*. And *we* – it seems that we want it worse and more than it ever was. Well-being as you think of it is no aim; to us it seems more like an *end* – a finish.[4]

Coming from someone, e.g. the slave-moralist, for whom things like public spirit were the important virtues, such views would seem strange and perverse. On the other hand, when we realise that Nietzsche saw suffering as a means to those things that he regarded as having supreme importance,

---
[1] Nietzsche, op. cit., p. 121.   [2] Ibid., p. 127.
[3] Whether he was right to think this is another matter. It could be argued that Nietzsche was mistaken to suppose that humble or pious actions require no strength of character or deep feelings.
[4] *Beyond Good and Evil*, p. 151.

artistic sensitivity, courage, and so on, we see that even this could be a moral view.

I have now described two ways in which we might interpret Nietzsche's attacks on slave-morality. What seems to emerge is that, whichever we choose, his views are intelligible only because he is able to support them with reasons which have some sort of connection with accepted moral considerations. This is what distinguishes the views of a revolutionary like Nietzsche from those of a maniac who completely disregards what is accepted as relevant in morality. The latter's statements *will* be literally incomprehensible.

However, I have also tried to make it clear that I do not wish to deny the important differences which Chekhov's maxim[1] brings out. For, although there must be points of contact between the revolutionary and the monk, there are also crucial differences. The monk typifies adherence to a certain scale of values. The rebel typifies rejection of this scale of values. But his purpose in rejecting it is to draw attention to other values to which he attaches importance, and which he feels are in danger of being ignored. Camus once remarked:

> It would be impossible to over-emphasise the passionate affirmation that underlies the act of revolt and which distinguishes it from resentment. Rebellion, though apparently negative since it creates nothing, is profoundly positive in that it reveals the part of man which must always be defended.[2]

What I have been trying to show is that only in so far as a revolution is based on the affirmation of moral values which are capable of being understood by others, can it have any meaning, even for the revolutionary himself. Unless this is so, not even negative criticism is possible.

It is important to emphasise this point, for in drawing attention to the role that tradition plays in the sphere of morality (and in any human activity), I may be taken to be

---

[1] See chapter 4, p. 39. [2] *The Rebel*, p. 25.

offering some sort of disguised plea for the *status quo*, which is far from my purpose. Part of the difficulty arises because the word 'tradition' is not always used in the same way. Often it is used to signify the customary behaviour of some particular society or of some particular age (think of its use in phrases like 'the Catholic tradition' or 'traditional skills'). In this sense, a 'defence of tradition' would be a defence of a particular scale of values, and in this sense the revolutionary is certainly not bound by tradition. Of course, there are many who feel that a departure from tradition, even in this sense, should be discouraged. Perhaps they see in change some sort of disregard for the beliefs of one's forebears ('What was good enough for my father is good enough for me'). Or perhaps they are of the opinion that the disadvantages of a revolution always outweigh the advantages. This would be a perfectly intelligible moral position. But it would be a moral position and not a philosophical one.

As I have been using the word, however, to talk of 'tradition' is not a way of referring to some particular set of beliefs. I can perhaps illustrate my use of the term by the way in which we talk of 'the scientific tradition'. It is sometimes said that certain procedures – say, the techniques of psycho-analysis – are not in keeping with the scientific tradition. Someone who wished to show that this was so might, for example, point out that many of the pronouncements of psycho-analysts are impervious to empirical confirmation or falsification (cf. Freud's remark, 'My theories are proved on the couch. They do not require experimental evidence').[1] Their purpose would be to show that the methods of psycho-analysis violate certain scientific principles. And this gives us a clue to what is meant by the phrase 'scientific tradition'. It refers not to any set of established theories, but rather to certain principles or standards which govern the procedures of scientists.

Of course, these principles do not form any finite, rigidly defined set. No one could formulate the principles which any procedure would have to conform to in order to be

[1] Quoted in Eysenck, *Fact and Fiction in Psychology*, p. 131.

called scientific, for this would be to treat 'science' as a closed concept, and would exclude the possibility of any scientific development. But this does not mean that we have any difficulty in saying that certain procedures could *not* be called scientific, for the possibility of calling a procedure scientific will depend on its relation to what has been done in the past. It must be possible to see the principles governing its use as developments of already established principles.

Now I think that this shows the sense in which even the rebel cannot ignore tradition. For there are certain principles (even if we are unable to formulate them) which enable us to draw a limit to what can count as a moral judgement. But we must avoid the mistake of equating 'tradition' with any finite set of moral standards, with, e.g. the *status quo*. For to do this *would* be to rule out the possibility of moral revolution. Tradition, in the sense in which I have been using the term, does not decide the moral beliefs which a man holds, but places a limit upon what it is intelligible to offer as a moral belief. To draw attention to this is a purely philosophical matter.

PART II
Moral Arguments

6
'Is' and 'Ought'

My intention in the first section of this monograph has been to show that the accounts of Hare and Mrs. Foot both offer misleading answers to the question: Are there any rules governing what counts as a moral reason? And in the preceding chapters I have tried to offer a third alternative and to defend it against some central objections. As yet I have, however, paid little attention to what might be thought to be the most important of the issues involved, namely the role which reasons play in moral argument. And if I am to pursue the arguments of the preceding chapters any further, this is an omission which must now be rectified. Let us begin by asking why this has been felt to present a problem for moral philosophy.

Hare and Mrs. Foot share with the majority of their contemporaries a certain picture of moral argument. On this view moral argument is seen as a process by which factual reasons are adduced in support of a moral conclusion. For example, suppose that I am asked to justify my condemnation of a certain person's character. I shall do so by indicating certain aspects of his behaviour. I may point out that he is kind to his parents, never refuses to help those less fortunate than himself, shows respect to his wife, and so on. Now, often these criteria of moral goodness will be factual. That is to say, there will be definite empirical tests for deciding their truth or falsity. Someone can only be said to help the needy if he does certain things, gives money to charity for instance, or forgives his debtors. The paradigm of a moral reason is held to be a factual statement of this kind.

True, my reasons for calling a man good will not always be of this sort. Often they will include non-factual assertions like 'He is upright', and this might seem to spoil the neatness of the picture which we are offered. But in fact it does not. For in such cases the reasons will themselves be moral judgements to be defended, if necessary, by reference to further statements of fact. Ultimately all moral valuations are based on statements of fact.

Now, if we accept this picture, difficulties immediately arise, for while moral valuations may be *based on* statements of fact, many philosophers have wished to deny that they are *reducible to* statements of fact. The relation between 'He is a good man' and 'He is courageous' or 'He is temperate' does not appear to be one of identity of meaning. We can give many different reasons for calling a man good (although, as I have tried to show, not anything that a man chooses to say will count as a reason), and if in each case 'good' just meant 'courageous' or 'temperate' or 'helpful', we should have to conclude that it was so ambiguous as to be quite meaningless. On the other hand, if we do not want to say that the relationship is one of identity of meaning, we seem to be presented with a gap between facts and values which requires to be bridged.

It is the main aim of the two accounts of morality which I am considering to show how this is to be done, that is, to show how it is possible for factual reasons to provide a foundation for moral (or, more generally, evaluative) conclusions.

Hare's account is best summarised in his own words. On p. 145 of *The Language of Morals* he tells us that the relation between the judgement that a man is a good man and the reasons for calling him good is that

> a statement of the characteristics of the man (the minor or factual premiss) *together with* a specification of a standard for judging him morally (the major premiss) entails a moral judgement upon him.

'Is' and 'Ought'

Hare construes a moral argument as a syllogism. In order to validate the inference from factual reasons to evaluative conclusion, an evaluative major premiss must be introduced. Moral argument then becomes a case of straightforward textbook inference.

On Mrs. Foot's account the inference in question holds not because of any suppressed major premiss ('All courageous, temperate men are good'), but because of 'the things that courage and temperance are'.[1] By this she does not mean that, to say that someone is courageous or temperate is already to make a value-judgement, in which case to say that someone possessed these characteristics would already presuppose that they were good. On the contrary, she believes that to call someone courageous is to make a purely factual assertion. If 'the facts have been accepted – say that x is the kind of man who will climb a dangerous mountain, beard an irascible employer for a rise in pay, and in general face the fearful for the sake of something that he thinks worthwhile',[2] then it would be unintelligible to refuse to admit that he was a courageous man. The connection between courage and goodness on Mrs. Foot's account (even though it still requires investigation) begins to become clear when we realise that courage is a means to an end. To see this is to see that it is necessarily a good thing.

From the brief sketch which I have given above, these two accounts may seem to present very different pictures of the relation between factual reasons and moral conclusions, between 'is' and 'ought'. In many ways they do, for while Mrs. Foot maintains that moral judgements can be reduced to factual judgements, this is precisely what Hare denies. But what I want to emphasise is that both share one crucial assumption. Let me try to explain this.

As we have seen, like Mrs. Foot, Hare holds that when we make a moral judgement, we do so on the basis of certain factual criteria. For example, we say that a man is good because he shows courage, because he goes to church, and so on. It is, however, central to his theory that 'X is good'

[1] 'Moral Beliefs', p. 98.   [2] Ibid., p. 98.

cannot just mean 'X shows courage, goes to church, etc.' X's goodness does not consist in any set of facts about him, however extensive. Unfortunately, this leads Hare to assume that it must consist in these facts *plus* something else over and above these facts. To him these seem the only possibilities. Either (i) the facts alone justify a moral judgement, or (ii) the facts plus some other element do so. And given that the first alternative is ruled out, Hare concludes that the task of moral philosophy must be that of elucidating the nature of this extra element.

That this is a fair representation of Hare's line of thought will become clear if we consider the following passage:

> If a parson says of a girl that she is a good girl, we can form a shrewd idea of what description she is.... It is therefore easy to fall into the error of supposing that by calling her a good girl, the parson means simply that she has these descriptive characteristics . . . but it is to be hoped that this is not all that he means. He also means to commend her for having them; and this part of his meaning is primary.[1]

What Hare tries to do here is to explain moral argument by introducing an element of commendation or evaluation. For, by themselves, descriptive criteria are insufficient to justify a moral judgement. They do so only in conjunction with an element of commendation. Moreover, this commendation is best expressed in the form of a major premiss in a syllogism, for this brings out its crucial role in a moral argument. Without it, moral arguments become broken-backed syllogisms.

When we turn to consider Mrs. Foot's account, we find many important differences. In particular Mrs. Foot rejects the notion of any general gap between facts and values such as is central to Hare's account. Nevertheless, there is one important similarity, for both assume that the justifications which men give for their moral judgements are in some way insufficient. For example, Mrs. Foot would agree with Hare that, as it stands, the argument from a girl's having certain

---

[1] *The Language of Morals*, p. 146.

characteristics to her being a good girl is incomplete. Certainly she would deny his claim that what it lacks is any element of commendation. For she would maintain that what is missing is the assertion that such characteristics are conducive to human good. My point is that both take for granted the necessity for some extra element beyond the reasons which men normally give, in order to justify their conclusions.

In this they are by no means alone. The majority of moral theories can be seen as attempts to find a middle term which will connect reasons and conclusion in a moral argument.

The emotivists, for instance, thought that they had discovered this in the expression of approval or condemnation:

> Thus, if I say to someone, 'You acted wrongly in stealing that money', I am not saying any more than if I had said simply, 'You stole that money'. In adding that this action is wrong, I am not making any further statement about it. I am simply evincing my moral disapproval of it.[1]

Again, the early utilitarians, like Mrs. Foot, sought the connection in the end which all men pursue,[2] although they differed from her in what they conceived this end to be. What I want to emphasise is that the same assumption characterises the work of all these philosophers. The factual reasons which men give can be relevant to the moral judgements which they make only through the mediation of some third element.

It seems to me that this approach to the problems facing the moral philosopher is a fruitless one. I do not think that moral argument can be explained as a process of linking reason and conclusion by some elusive extra element. Nor do I see why such an explanation should be thought to be necessary, why it should be thought to be the task of moral philosophy to interpret moral arguments as disguised

[1] A. J. Ayer, *Language, Truth and Logic*, p. 107.
[2] Mrs. Foot's recent remarks in the Introduction to *Theories of Ethics* would seem to imply that her views about the nature of this end have changed to some extent.

Moral Reasoning

syllogisms or as disguised means-end arguments. My purpose in the remainder of this essay will be to explain the alternative to these views.

I want to begin by comparing two examples of value-judgements, one from outside morality and the other a moral judgement.

1. During a game of chess[1] one player (A) moves his Queen's Bishop to Queen's Bishop 6, and in this way places his opponent's King in checkmate. Both agree that this was the right move to make. So would anyone who understood chess. In this case then, 'The right move' and 'Queen's Bishop to QB6' apply to the same move. Yet the two phrases certainly do not mean the same. We can think of circumstances in which this would have been the wrong move to make, or not even a legitimate move at all, e.g. where A's King is itself in check.

2. Graham Greene's *The Heart of the Matter* contains an account of the attitudes of a group of Catholics and non-Catholics towards two suicides, that of a Catholic police commissioner, Scobie, and that of the non-Catholic Pemberton. To a large extent the Catholics are agreed in their attitudes. At the very least they agree that what Scobie and Pemberton did was wrong. For example, when it is discovered that Scobie caused his own death by taking an overdose of drugs, both his wife and their priest, Father Rank, condemn his action. Scobie himself felt that what he intended to do was a matter for condemnation. But 'causing one's own death by an overdose of drugs' does not always mean 'doing what is wrong'. For it would be quite intelligible to say that this was the right thing to do in certain circumstances.

Now, it seems to me that there is some sort of analogy between the two examples which I have chosen, despite the important differences between them, and I want to begin by considering the relationship between facts and values in the former. The question which we have to ask is: How is it

---

[1] This example was suggested to me by Max Black's article, 'The Gap between "Is" and "Should" '. But I think that in some ways Black makes an illegitimate use of it.

possible for someone to argue from the factual statement that A has moved his Queen's Bishop to QB6, to the evaluative judgement that A has made the right move.

And, as I have said, we seem to be faced with a dilemma. In saying that a move with such-and-such characteristics is the right move, we are saying either that the move has these characteristics and nothing else, or we are saying that it has these characteristics and something else (commending it, pointing out that it is a means to some end). Furthermore, if, as Hare and Mrs. Foot agree, the first alternative is untenable, we really seem to be committed to the second.

These difficulties arise in the first place because we try to lift the inference out of its context. It is as if we were saying: Ignore the fact that what is being discussed is a move in a game of chess. Forget that the value-judgement in question is made by chess-players. Just explain how the two would be connected if they did not occur in this sort of context. And of course we find that what we have been asked to do is impossible. Certainly the conclusion does not follow from the facts alone (if this means that the relation between them cannot be understood independently of the context in which the two occur). But this does not necessitate the introduction of any extra elements. Both the conclusion and the reasons can be understood only when we see them as part of the activity of playing chess. And within such a context the judgement that a certain move would be the right one to make, follows solely from the description of this move as 'Queen's Bishop to QB6'.

True, given *another* context and the conclusion may not follow. Suppose, to take another of Max Black's examples, that the other player (B) is in such a dangerous state of health that 'the shock of being mated by an inferior player would kill him'.[1] In these sort of circumstances it is by no means clear that the mating-move will be the right one to make. But the reason why this is so is that we are no longer merely concerned with a move in a chess-game, but with an action on the plane of morality, and here different considerations

[1] 'The Gap between "Is" and "Should"', p. 175.

Moral Reasoning

become relevant. But within the context of a chess-game the facts bind the participants to an evaluative conclusion.

To those who, like Hare, are concerned to emphasise the fundamental differences between statements of fact and judgements of value, both within morality and elsewhere, the above may not seem a promising line of argument. Surely, it will be objected, there can be no valid inference from facts to values, even *within* a context such as the activity of playing chess. For even here, how can a purely neutral description of the movement of certain chess-pieces possibly constitute a justification for the assertion that the right move has been made? Surely the gap between 'is' and 'ought' (or 'right') is just as insurmountable here as elsewhere.

And certainly I do not wish to pretend that a purely neutral description could ever justify an evaluative judgement. What has to be challenged is the suggestion that a statement like 'A moved his Queen's Bishop to QB6' *is* a 'purely neutral description'. It is quite unlike such statements as 'The cat sat on the mat' or 'He always wears a green suit', both of which might be said, with some justification, to fall into this category. For in saying that A's move is a move in a chess-game, we already presuppose certain conventions and standards (including those which govern what is to count as a move in a chess-game in the first place). No doubt it would be quite possible to describe A's move in purely neutral terms: A moved a piece of carved ivory from one position on a board composed of thirty-two alternating black and white squares to another position. No evaluative conclusion would follow from such a description. But neither would it give any idea of the significance of the move in a game of chess. Nor would a chess-player use such a description. What he would say is that A moved his Queen's Bishop to QB6. And such a person would then understand this move as (in certain circumstances) the right one to make. The reason why the facts bind participants in a chess-game to the same conclusion is that for them the facts already possess evaluative import. They are not *just* facts.

'Is' and 'Ought'

We must now enquire whether this example has any relevance to morality. And here we shall have to be careful. For it does not, I think, have the sort of relevance that many people have thought it to have. Many philosophers, wishing to deny the possibility of ultimate moral disagreements ('moral breakdowns'), have seized upon the example of inferences from fact to value made within games like chess, in the mistaken belief that this will help their case. Black himself does so. After correctly noting that in a chess-game the facts may give a conclusive reason for accepting a value-judgement, Black assumes that there are therefore grounds for supposing that moral conclusions are also related to factual reasons in a precisely analogous way. Moreover, he seems to think that in such a case the inference would hold regardless of anyone's moral beliefs, so that 'given that a moral conclusion is to be drawn we have no choice as to which conclusion it shall be'.[1] Just as in chess anyone accepting the facts of the case is committed to drawing a certain conclusion, so in morality anyone accepting the facts of the case is committed to a particular moral judgement. On this view, moral disagreement can stem only from ignorance of fact or lack of understanding.

I have already given reasons for supposing that the sort of approach exemplified by Black's article is fundamentally misconceived. At present I am concerned only to draw attention to one of the defects in his argument. This arises, not merely because Black tries to draw an analogy between moral justification and the sort of justification which is offered in a chess-game, but because of the *particular sort* of analogy which he tries to draw. To see that this is so, let us ask whether it would be possible to draw the same sort of inferences in chess as Black does if there were more than one variant of the game. Would Black's account still apply?

Suppose, for instance, that there is a type of chess where the mating-move, instead of winning a game for a player, brings about a draw (much as the position called 'stalemate' does in orthodox chess) and that games are won and lost in a

[1] 'The Gap between "Is" and "Should" ', p. 178.

different manner altogether. And suppose that a bystander (C) is watching A and B playing a game which has reached exactly the same stage as the game in Black's example. C says to A, 'The right move would be Queen's Bishop to QB6'. Is this so?

Clearly whether this is the right move or not will depend on which game A and B are playing. If they are playing orthodox chess, then C would be right. If they are playing the other variant then he would probably not be.

The point of drawing attention to this hypothetical situation is that it is in some ways similar to what actually happens in the field of morality. Several people may discuss moral problems without it necessarily following that they are playing the same 'moral game'. There are *many* moralities, and because members of one morality draw a particular inference, we cannot just assume *a priori* that those in another morality will do the same. We have to look to see whether they do. This is why Black is wrong to think that there can be any straightforward transition from a game of chess to morality in general.

Nevertheless, what I want to suggest is that there is a reasonably close analogy between the process of justification which is offered in a game of chess and that which is offered within a *particular* moral code. We saw earlier that the idea that an argument from 'A moved his Queen's Bishop to QB6' to 'A made the right move' is in some way incomplete, arises chiefly because philosophers have tried to ignore the context in which these judgements occur. If we now turn to the second of our examples, I think that we shall find that the same is true here. Mrs. Scobie and Father Rank agree in regarding Scobie's killing himself as sufficient grounds for condemning him, because they share the same viewpoint – that of a Catholic morality. Within this viewpoint no reference to an element of evaluation or to the end of morality is required. To draw attention to the fact that Scobie took an overdose of drugs commits one to the moral judgement that what he did was wrong.

Once again, however, the inference is possible only

'Is' and 'Ought'

because, within the context of a Catholic morality, this alleged statement of fact is not *just* a statement of fact. To represent 'Scobie took an overdose of drugs' as an uncommitted description of certain physical movements robs it of the particular significance which it has for a Catholic. If we are to call this a fact, we must recognise that for Father Rank and Mrs. Scobie the fact is already endowed with moral import.

7
Moral Viewpoints and Our Ideas of Reality

In the foregoing chapter, I suggested that the traditional dichotomy of facts and values need present the moral philosopher with no difficulty, since within a particular morality no such general distinction can be made. There the facts already possess moral import, for any significance which they may have for a man is determined by the central concepts of his moral code, by his values. This must now be explained more fully.

Since I wish to argue that the traditional views rest on a fallacious idea of the relation between two terms, (i) facts and (ii) values, it will be convenient to regard my own view as differing from them in two ways; that is (*a*) in its account of the nature of a man's values, those concepts which constitute his moral outlook, and (*b*) in its account of the role which the facts play in morality. I intend to devote the following two chapters to a consideration of each of these aspects in turn.

Earlier in this thesis[1] I pointed out that there are certain concepts which may be regarded as constitutive of morality, in that it is by reference to them that ultimate moral justifications are offered. Now the view which I proposed in the last chapter is partly a view about the role of these concepts in a

[1] See chapter 4, pp. 42–46.

man's life. For what I am arguing is that they decide what significance the facts can have for us, that is to say, determine our ideas of reality.

One way in which we may indicate how this account diverges from the views of Hare and Mrs. Foot is by considering what it would mean for a man to reject these concepts, what such a rejection would involve. Would it, for instance, make sense to suppose that a man brought up to regard suicide, murder and adultery as evils, might somehow get outside these values and ask himself whether they were not perhaps virtues? It should be clear that on my account such a question would be incoherent. I am maintaining that the events in a man's life, the decisions he makes, his problems and judgements, have the significance for him that they do, only by reference to his moral viewpoint. So it is by no means clear what it could mean to suppose that he might simply set himself to question the worth of this viewpoint.

A quite different view is suggested by the following passage:

> A man who asked himself seriously whether he should continue with a policy of truth-telling and promise-keeping, (not that anyone does), would be like a doctor who proposed to set aside the most fundamental items of medical knowledge and build up his science from scratch. That sort of performance is suitable for philosophers, but altogether too dangerous for practical men.[1]

On this view, the reason why 'practical men' are not assailed by doubts about the value of honesty and promise-keeping is that any way of life which did not place a premium on these values would be unlikely to meet with much success. Nevertheless, Walsh clearly thinks that there is room for doubt, that, although dangerous, such doubts would be intelligible. Furthermore, since he is using 'honesty' and 'promise-keeping' as examples, he clearly intends his remarks to apply quite generally. Just as a doctor might decide to suspend all of his medical beliefs and then

[1] W. H. Walsh, 'Moral Authority and Moral Choice', p. 20.

determine by examining the facts, which he wished to adopt and which reject, so the moral agent may suspend his moral beliefs and decide on the basis of the facts which are worthy of acceptance, although Walsh would no doubt regard such a performance as doubly dangerous.

Both Hare and Mrs. Foot would, I think, agree with Walsh's general point, although their reasons for doing so would differ. For Hare, a man's whole morality rests on what he calls a 'decision of principle'. Of course, by introducing the concept of a decision, Hare is not denying that many people simply acquiesce in the moral values of their parents or those concerned with their upbringing. Perhaps he would deplore this situation, but he realises that it is conceivable. His point is merely that any moral code rests on someone's decision, and that it is always possible for a man to decide to reject this code.

Mrs. Foot's account commits her to a position similar to Hare's in some respects. For her, morality is a technique for attaining a certain predetermined end. If lying is wrong then this is because it leads to various human evils. But that this is so can only be a matter of experience. It is quite conceivable that experience should teach us otherwise, and if this were to happen, we should then have to adopt a policy of lying. But, according to Mrs. Foot, Hare is wrong to suppose that this would be a matter for decision. In such a case it would no longer be open to us to decide whether to adopt dishonesty as one of our moral values. We should have no *choice* but to do so. In an extreme case it is conceivable that experience might *force* us to call in question our whole moral code.

I think that these sorts of view are radically mistaken, and that their errors may be traced to the language which is used to describe certain aspects of moral discourse. Hare and Mrs. Foot share (together with most other moral philosophers) the unfortunate tendency to refer to judgements like 'Murder is wrong' or 'One ought to tell the truth' as 'moral principles' or 'moral beliefs'. Moreover, they do so under the mistaken impression that this terminology requires no justification. Hare, for example, takes it for granted that any judgement of the form 'X is wrong' is to be regarded as a 'principle of conduct'.

But, in fact, this use of the terms 'principle' and 'belief' is not just highly controversial. It carries with it a false suggestion. For it neglects the fundamental role of such judgements in a man's life and implies that his so-called 'moral principles' and 'moral beliefs' are open to just the sorts of questioning and change whose possibility I am denying. To see this we shall have to consider some less controversial instances of principles and beliefs, in order, if possible, to discover their salient features.

Let us begin with 'principle'. This appears in a fairly wide range of contexts, some of which are moral (as, for example, when someone says, 'I make it a matter of principle never to disagree with my wife' or refers to another person as 'unprincipled'). But it is used most characteristically to designate those general rules which enable us to attain competence in human activities such as playing golf or driving a car. Thus, for instance, we speak of 'Avoid body sway when teeing off' as a principle of golf, or of 'Depress clutch before changing gear' as a principle of driving.

Now the important thing to note about these sorts of principles is that they are necessarily subject to modification and change in the light of experience, or as a result of changing conditions. For example, a change in the maximum size of golf-courses, or in the characteristics of golf-balls, would almost certainly bring about a change in the principles which coaches teach their pupils. Or again, if cars were introduced which required no gear-box, then the principle 'Depress clutch before changing gear' would become redundant.

This applies quite generally to such principles. No matter how fundamental they may be, it is always possible to imagine circumstances in which we should be forced to reject them. We see why this is so when we realise that the principles of golf or of driving have a purpose. They are rules-of-thumb to enable a man to play golf competently or drive safely, without having to start from scratch each time he picks up a golf-club or switches on the ignition. And it is only in so far as they conduce to their respective ends that they have any meaning for us. Consequently, it is quite conceivable that there should be a situation in which we should be forced to adopt a wholly different set of principles in order to achieve our desired ends.

If we now turn to consider a typical set of beliefs, for instance medical beliefs, we find one important difference. For beliefs, unlike principles, do not presuppose any reference to the notion of an end. When a doctor tells us that he believes that one of his patients has glandular fever, it would be meaningless to say that he has a purpose in doing so. If we ask him, 'Why do you believe that?' we do not mean 'What do you hope to achieve by believing that?' but rather 'What evidence have you for your belief?'

But there are also important similarities between principle and beliefs.[1] Medical beliefs, like the principles of golf, depend on something external to themselves. For it is part of what we mean by calling something a belief that it is dependent on experience, and that on the basis of our experience we may be required to reject it. For example, the doctor who diagnoses his patient's illness as glandular fever knows very well what would lead him to reject this belief, namely the discovery that his patient's blood count is normal. And, while it is unlikely, it is possible that all his medical beliefs should suffer the same fate. None of them is sacrosanct, for if it were we should not call it a belief but a dogma.

When we speak of a judgement as a 'belief' or a 'principle' then we presuppose some standard in terms of which a belief can be true or false, a principle adequate or inadequate. It is this standard which makes it meaningful to speak of a man changing or questioning his principles or beliefs.

Unfortunately, by speaking of moral conventions like honesty and promise-keeping as 'principles, or 'beliefs',

[1] This, of course, is to be expected, since to adhere to a principle is to hold a belief about the best way of attaining a certain end.

philosophers have caused confusion. For they have been led to suppose that a man's moral code is subject to just the sort of change which might, in certain circumstances, characterise the principles of driving. Indeed, they are logically committed to this supposition. For we regard a principle or a belief which is *not* amenable to change in the light of experience as a dogma or a prejudice. And this is something essentially irrational.

This is not, of course, meant to imply that the principles governing human activities *do* often change in any radical fashion. The principles of horse-riding, for instance, are the result of centuries of experience in this field. If someone were to suggest that horsemen would do better to adopt a different posture in the saddle, or to hold the reins in a different way, we should be entitled to view this suggestion with suspicion. Nevertheless, we must always bear in mind that such a change may, in certain circumstances, be necessary. At the turn of the century, an American jockey named Tod Sloan arrived in England to demonstrate a completely new racing style.[1] Instead of sitting upright in the saddle like British jockeys he crouched up against his mount's neck. British critics were dubious, but when Sloan proceeded to defeat all British opposition on the racecourse, they had to admit that the traditional style of racing was inadequate to this new challenge. For a jockey to have continued to ride in this way simply on the grounds that he had learned by the principle 'Sit up in the saddle' and didn't intend to change would have been incomprehensible.

Consequently, if we maintain, as I am doing, that our fundamental ideas of right and wrong cannot be questioned and changed in the same way as can the principles of horse-riding, and yet continue to talk as if a man's moral code were nevertheless just a collection of principles, we are liable to fall into the mistake of equating morality and prejudice.

The remedy for this is to realise that honesty and promise-keeping, justice and integrity, are not principles to enable the virtuous man to achieve some end, not tools for dealing

[1] I owe this example to Professor Wisdom (*Paradox and Discovery*, p. 146).

with experience, but have a quite different part to play in his life. Perhaps we can best illustrate this difference by comparing the function of principles like the principles of driving in practical arguments, and that of concepts like honesty in moral arguments.

Consider the following arguments:

A: You ought to change into second gear when you take such a tight corner as that.

B: But I had complete control of the car in third gear, and if I had changed down I shouldn't have had time to signal to the car behind. It's more important to give adequate signals.

A: Well, I say that a driver ought always to make sure that he's in the right gear. You couldn't see round that corner and it might have been tighter than you expected.

Now compare this with a typical moral argument:

Solicitor: I advise you to make over your property to your wife and children. This is quite legal and they will avoid having to pay death duties.

Client: I'm afraid that I couldn't do that. Even if it is within the law, I regard it as dishonest.

Solicitor: But you have worked all your life to provide for your family. Surely it's unjust that a government should take it all from them when you die.

Now, in both of these arguments the disputants are discussing which of two alternatives should be adopted. But there is an important difference. In the first example A and B disagree *about* which principles a driver should adopt. A says that he should adhere to the principle 'Change down before tight corners'. B says that the principle 'Always give adequate signals' is more important. But an understanding of the dispute does not depend on an understanding of the principles in question. A non-driver listening to A and B arguing could give some account of what was going on, even if he had no idea of what 'changing gear' and 'giving signals' involved. For he would be able to explain that A and B were discussing the best way of attaining a certain end, namely cornering safely.

The second argument involves considerations like 'honesty' and 'justice'. But these play a quite different part from the principles in the first example. For the parties do not disagree *about* honesty and justice. Indeed, we might say that their dispute is to be understood *in terms of* these concepts. It would be quite impossible for anyone who did not understand what was meant by 'honesty' and 'justice', or who did not understand that honesty and justice were virtues, to make any sense of the argument. Unless they understood that an action's being dishonest is a ground for condemning it, they would find the client's remarks unintelligible. Nor would they understand anything that the solicitor said, unless they regarded justice as a virtue. The very possibility of the solicitor and his client disagreeing presupposes that there is no disagreement over honesty and justice. For these concepts provide the standard by which each can understand and criticise the other's moral judgements. It follows that they are not themselves to be regarded as principles or beliefs.

We can illustrate this point in a different way by indicating a further difference between the two examples. It will be noticed that in the first argument statements like 'It is better to change down before tight corners' and 'One ought always to give adequate signals' play an important part. They form the subject-matter of the dispute, and we can imagine that throughout it A and B would often have occasion to make such judgements. By contrast, I should not want to say that judgements like 'Honesty is good' or 'One ought to be just' ever feature in moral discourse. Nor is this merely because they are so obvious that no normal person would bother to draw attention to them (as might be said of the principle 'You must hold the wheel when driving'). Rather it is because we should have difficulty understanding someone who did say these sort of things, for they are never in dispute.

To this it may be objected that we do sometimes address

such remarks to children. This objection would, of course, be correct. Such phrases occur in moral instruction. And it may be illuminating to compare them with other judgements used only in teaching a child. I am thinking of judgements like 'One is a number' or 'Yellow is a colour'. When we say this sort of thing to a child, we are explaining the role of a concept in language. But to explain that 1 is a number, is not to say anything about (the number) 1. Nor does it tell us anything about yellow to say that it is a colour (nothing that you could verify by observation, or by consulting an artist). These are not the sort of things that anyone who had learned to count or to use colour-words would say. But if we are to maintain that 'One is a number' plays a part in the sphere of mathematics, we must be quite clear that it plays a quite different part from, say:

$$1 = 1 \times \tfrac{1}{2} \times 2$$
or
$$1 = \tfrac{2}{3} + \tfrac{2}{3} - \tfrac{1}{3}$$

We cannot even imagine mathematicians arguing whether 1 is a number or not. For we cannot imagine *any* mathematical disagreement which does not presuppose this.

Now 'Honesty is good' is in many ways similar. Unlike, e.g., 'It always pays to tell the truth', it says nothing about honesty. Rather it shows us the role which the concept of honesty plays in a morality, just as 'Promises ought to be kept' and 'Murder is an evil' show the role which these concepts play in morality. Such judgements form the basis for any moral agreement or disagreement, for they have a place among the rules according to which moral discourse can take place. And this is why they are so rarely explicitly stated in moral arguments. Those philosophers who have talked as if moral agents continually said such things have been misled by thinking of them as principles.

What I hope these points bring out is that there is something suspicious in the idea of a man suspending his acceptance of the central concepts in his moral code in order to decide, by reference to the facts, whether or not to retain them. When Mill says of Bentham 'that murder, incendiarism, robbery are mischievous actions, he will not take for granted without proof',[1] he is describing a *senseless* doubt, as senseless as, for instance, Descartes' doubts about the testimony of the senses. It would be intelligible only if judgements embodying these concepts were principles or beliefs, and were themselves open to criticism from some external standard. But, as we have seen, they are not. They are the standard on which any criticism must be based. To suppose that they can be questioned in this way is not like supposing that a golfer might decide to question the principle 'Avoid body sway when teeing off'. It is more like supposing that he might ask whether he ought to hole the golf-ball. Someone who refused to hole the ball would not be playing golf. In the same way, someone who tried to reject concepts like honesty or justice would be rejecting the standard on which his own moral judgement was based. He would be playing a different moral game.

As it stands this account might seem to be open to crucial objections. What I have been maintaining is that whereas principles such as those of golf or of horse-riding are of their very nature subject to change in the light of experience, this is not true of the central concepts of a man's morality. For the latter, unlike the former, themselves determine what significance our experience has for us.

Unfortunately, by saying this, I may seem to be ignoring the extent to which a man's experience of life may bring about a change in his moral beliefs. For, in the field of morals, as in those of science, religion, and everyday empirical knowledge, we do undoubtedly speak of people learning from experience or gaining insight. Books like *The Way of All Flesh* or *Hard Times* exhibit certain kinds of moral development in detail. So, it will be said, if my argument is intended to exclude the possibility of such development taking place, it must necessarily contain some flaw.

My answer is that this is by no means my intention. All I have been trying to show is that certain concepts (like

[1] 'Bentham', p. 85

'honesty' and 'integrity') will occupy a fundamental role in a person's life. This does not mean that learning from experience is impossible; only that the sort of account of it implicit in the theories of Hare and Mrs. Foot must be mistaken. Such learning does not take place in independence of a man's ideas of what is right and wrong. I think that I can best explain where I differ from them by means of an example.

Camus' novel *The Plague* provides, in Tarron's explanation of his attitude to capital punishment, an illustration of one important way in which a man's views may be changed or modified by his experience. During a conversation with his friend Doctor Rieux, Tarron describes how, until his late teens, he had regarded the death-penalty as a quite natural aspect of law enforcement. He accepted that the taking of life was justified as a deterrent, 'inevitable for the building up of a new world in which murder would cease to be'.[1] However, his widening experience of life (seeing a man condemned to death in court, witnessing an execution) had a profound effect on Tarron. He became disgusted with

> that foul procedure whereby dirty mouths stinking of plague told a fettered man that he was going to die, and scientifically arranged things so that he should die, after nights and nights of mental torture while he waited to be murdered in cold blood [2]

As a result of his experiences, his views on capital punishment changed. 'I told myself that . . . nothing in the world would induce me to adopt any argument that justified such butcheries.'[3]

I should say that what Tarron learns from his experience is the consequences of certain ways of acting, consequences which he would otherwise not have considered. He learns the mental torture and human suffering which the death-penalty gives rise to. This is what we mean here when we say that he has matured or gained insight; and the effect of this increased insight is to make him reject his old beliefs about capital punishment. But one thing to note is that such a change occurs because the avoidance of human suffering was

[1] *The Plague*, p. 205.   [2] Ibid., p. 206.   [3] Ibid.

already a consideration of fundamental importance in Tarron's morality. If it were not, then the discovery that the institution of executing murderers leads to suffering would have left him unmoved. At least it would scarcely have led to the sort of change in Tarron's life which did in fact occur. For this change is a manifestation of his moral attitude, or his fundamental ideas of what is right and wrong.

The sort of learning from experience which Tarron describes is quite different from that which characterises other spheres of activity. A jockey who had learned that sitting back in the saddle prevented him from winning races and yet refused to change his style would, as we have seen, be acting unintelligibly. Yet we can easily imagine someone with the same experience of life as Tarron (even someone who has, in a superficial sense, had the same experiences as Tarron) whose beliefs about capital punishment remain unchanged. Like him, they are aware of its consequences, they possess the same degree of moral insight as he does, but *they* regard human suffering as a fitting punishment for taking the life of another. And since the difference between them is a moral difference, there does not seem to be anything that philosophy can say about it. Both know where capital punishment leads. There is no difference between them in that respect. But one thinks that that is where it ought to lead and the other does not.

This shows what is wrong with the suggestion that moral disputes, or evaluative disputes in general, should be settled by an appeal to a panel of experts.[1] It is, of course, completely artificial to speak of 'experts' or 'competent judges' in morality. For these terms can have a sense only where it also makes sense to talk of a standard of competence or expertise. We know, for example, what we mean by saying that a man is a competent clarinettist or an expert marksman. For we know what tests would determine whether or not he fell into these categories. A competent clarinettist produces a full, rounded

---

[1] Mill (*Utilitarianism*, pp. 12–15) says that the question, 'Which is the more valuable of two pleasures', is to be resolved by the decision of 'competent judges'.

tone, reads music with a certain amount of dexterity, and can finger fairly difficult passages. An expert marksman can hit the centre of the target, not just in perfect conditions, but in high winds or bad visibility. But it is difficult to know what could be meant by saying that there is such a standard in morality.

In fact, what Mill does is to introduce his own standard. He tells us that by 'competent judges' he means those who have had experience of the different kinds of pleasure in question. The experts in this sense are those who possess the sort of insight which stems from experience and which Tarron came to possess. Unfortunately, this creates even greater difficulties for Mill's theory. For, as we have seen, there is no reason to suppose that the 'experts' in this sense will agree in the judgements that they make. They will do so only if they share the same values. And the whole point of Mill's utilitarian doctrine is to secure agreement between *different* sets of values. It is evident that this can never be done by an appeal to 'competent judges'.

The point which I have been trying to make is that if we are to talk of a man learning from experience in the sphere of morality, we must be clear that the sense which he makes of his experience (and therefore what he learns) will depend on the central concepts of his moral code. Of course, what I have said should not be taken to imply that the way in which Tarron's views changed is the only possible way. In particular, when we speak of a man having been converted, or of his having 'come to see things in a different light' a far more radical change is usually involved. And it might be thought that here at least we are concerned with something which is more amenable to explanation on the lines suggested by Hare or Mrs. Foot.

But is this really so? Though the change in the convert's views may be a radical one, it is clear that it does not depend on a 'decision of principle' in Hare's sense. The convert does not simply decide to change his views, but rather comes to see that in some important way his views are wrong. To say of such a man that he had just decided to change his moral

Moral Viewpoints and Our Ideas of Reality

viewpoint would imply that for him the change had no deep significance, that it did not really matter.[1]

On the other hand, it may be confusing if we say (with Mrs. Foot) that experience *forces* the convert to change his views. For, as was true of Tarron, he is not forced to change them in the way that men are forced to change their principles when these are found not to pay. As we have seen, a principle or a belief is accepted only in so far as it is in agreement with the facts. When this is no longer the case then *no one* can rationally retain it. But if we say of the convert that he is forced to change his views, in order to deny the mistaken belief that he simply chooses to do so, then we must be clear that the important word here is 'he'. *He* is forced to change them, but for you and I it might be quite different. Nor are we being irrational if we find no cause for change in what he does. It is just that we do not see things in the way that he does.

The possibility of moral conversion does nothing to disprove my central claim that the significance of the facts is determined by a man's ideas of morality. When a man is converted, what happens is that his moral viewpoint itself changes in a fundamental way and he comes to attach a new significance to the facts. Certainly, he may be unable to give a reason for his new attitude in terms of his previous beliefs, in the way that Tarron can point to the avoidance of human suffering as the overriding factor in his change of heart. If he explains it all, he may say that he 'came to see what was really important' or that he 'came to see how things really were'. Nothing that I have said is intended to preclude this possibility. What I do wish to deny is that a man should reject his moral viewpoint as a whole, and then decide by reference to the facts what new one he should adopt. For it is only by reference to this viewpoint that the facts have any significance for him.

[1] Cf. my remarks on the suggestion that such changes in a man's views must be regarded as in some way arbitrary (chapter 9).

8
Facts and 'Pure' Facts

Chapter 7 of this essay was devoted to a consideration of one aspect of the traditional distinction between facts and values. There I tried to explain the respects in which my account of a man's moral values differs from those of Hare and Mrs. Foot. In the present chapter I turn to the other aspect of this distinction. My aim will be to examine the role which the facts play in moral reasoning.

As we have seen, most moral philosophers are agreed that particular moral judgements are to be defended by an appeal to factual considerations. Many would say that a judgement does not count as a moral judgement unless it can be so defended. I do not wish to deny this. My point is simply that it may well be misleading unless we consider closely what we mean by 'the facts' here. Let us begin with the example which I considered earlier, that of a Catholic who condemns a man for committing suicide. It seems to me that there are two false assumptions which a philosopher may make about this sort of case.

1. In the first place he may assume that the reasons which the Catholic gives for his moral judgement do not constitute a complete justification for it, and that they can do so only in conjunction with something else. Both Hare and Mrs. Foot make this assumption. On Hare's account the 'something else' is a major premiss. On Mrs. Foot's account it is a statement about the point (or purpose) of morality.

2. Hare and Mrs. Foot also assume that since we can

describe the Catholic in this example as making a moral judgement (X did wrong) on the basis of a factual statement (X committed suicide), we can also regard 'X committed suicide' as a *purely* factual statement. That is to say, they assume that, even for a Catholic, the judgement 'X committed suicide' is without moral import. In itself it is thought to have no more moral significance than the statement 'X smoked a Havana cigar'.

It is important to notice that there is a logical connection between these two assumptions. The first follows from the second. If the statement 'X committed suicide' has as little moral significance as 'X smoked a Havana cigar', then it will clearly give as little justification for the judgement 'X did wrong', i.e. no justification at all. And *prima facie* one would imagine that this gives a good reason for rejecting the view that 'X committed suicide' is a purely neutral (descriptive) statement. For surely, if we admit that for a Catholic this statement possesses moral import, then there is no longer any reason to doubt that it is a complete justification for the judgement 'X did wrong'.

But, for Hare at least, this answer will not do. Either, he maintains, the term 'suicide' is a purely factual term, in which case no moral judgement can be derived from it, or it is a moral term. But if it is a moral term, then the difficulty is merely pushed back a further stage. For we are left without any factual criteria for deciding where it is applicable. Furthermore, even if factual criteria could be given, we should once more be faced with the difficulty of deriving a moral judgement from them.[1]

This is a powerful objection, and one which is best dealt with by looking at the way in which the Catholic actually uses the term 'suicide'. Is it a purely descriptive term within the Catholic morality? Or does it have moral import? And if the latter is the case, does it follow that there is no morally neutral criterion for deciding where it is applicable?

In the first place, I think that it is at least clear that for those who share the Catholic viewpoint the judgement 'X

[1] See *Freedom and Reason*, pp. 208–13.

committed suicide' will have moral import. In Greene's *The Heart of the Matter*, Scobie's action is correctly described as 'suicide'. And some people (certain Protestants, for example) might describe it in this way without committing themselves to a moral judgement. But for a Catholic this would not be so. When Father Rank, the Catholic priest, admits that Scobie has taken his own life, he is not just describing Scobie's action. He is passing judgement upon it. It would be quite superfluous for him to add that this action is wrong. Suicide *is* one of the ways in which a Catholic can do wrong.

Nevertheless, it would be quite misleading to suggest that 'suicide' is not a factual term. The Catholic's criteria for calling an action 'suicide' are just the same as those of anyone else. The conversation at Fellowes' dinner party shows this. Several guests are discussing Pemberton's death. Both Scobie and his host accept just the same facts as evidence for the claim that Pemberton committed suicide (he strangled himself with a length of cord attached to a picture-hanger); nevertheless they judge his action differently. For Fellowes it is clear that 'a chap's got the right to take his own life'.[1] For Scobie suicide is 'the unforgivable sin'.[2] But this is not because they disagree over the facts, but because the facts have a different significance for them. If their criteria for suicide were not the same, then any moral disagreement would be impossible. For in saying that Pemberton committed suicide, they would not even be saying the same thing.

This seems to imply that a Catholic does not draw Hare's distinction between factual and moral judgements when he talks about suicide. We can, if we wish, call 'Scobie committed suicide' a moral judgement, as long as we realise that there can be no moral disagreement over its application, or we can say that it is a factual statement, if we recognise that within the context of a Catholic morality it carries moral import. What we cannot do is to draw a rigid distinction between the two.

Philosophers have tended to ignore this because they have

[1] *The Heart of the Matter*, p. 185.   [2] Ibid., p. 186.

failed to consider the circumstances in which a child would learn the use of such statements. They have talked as if we learn what suicide, murder or lying are, without learning the moral significance which these concepts have in our society. But a little reflection will show that this is not so. We do not learn the meaning of these terms in morally neutral situations, simply because the people by whom we are taught themselves possess certain values. They do not merely describe actions as 'murder', 'suicide', or 'lying', but also react to them in characteristic ways.

This becomes apparent if we examine a concept such as that of greed. Within our society greed, particularly in the somewhat limited sense in which it is equated with gluttony, is fairly uniformly condemned. We punish greedy children, express disapproval of those in whom this trait has persisted into adult life, and so on. Consequently, when a child learns to use this term, though he learns it as a descriptive term, he also learns that his parents and teachers will react to greed in certain ways. And he learns to react in these ways himself. When Johnny takes the largest apple from the plate, or demands his sister's apple as well as his own, his mother explains to him that these actions are greedy. But unless she regards them as praiseworthy, or for some reason conceals her feelings, she does not *just* describe them as 'greed'. Rather she does so in such a way as to make clear that a moral offence is involved, perhaps by adopting a tone of rebuke ('Oh, you *greedy* child'), perhaps by accompanying her words with some kind of punishment. It is even more likely that Johnny is told *that* he has done wrong, and only afterwards *why* he has done wrong ('Don't do that, Johnny.' 'Why not?' 'Because it's greedy').

Johnny will have to hear the word 'greed' in a great many sorts of situation before he learns to use it correctly. We should not say that he knew its meaning if he could apply it only to the case of taking the largest apple. But he will probably never hear it used with anything but a disapproving tone. The result of this is that this term, and to a perhaps even greater extent terms like 'murder' or 'suicide', come to possess for him what some philosophers have called 'emotive force', or what I should prefer to call 'moral import'. Of course, this is not meant to imply that, for him, these are not descriptive terms. It is intended to draw attention to the way in which the learning of facts and values goes side by side within a moral code.

Theorists have neglected this point largely because they have tended to think of moral instruction, on the analogy of learning a skill, as a process whereby a child is acquainted with a list of principles. Hare makes this explicit:

> Without principles, most kinds of teaching would be impossible, for what we learn is in most cases a principle. In particular when we learn to *do* something, what we learn is always a principle. . . . The point is . . . that to learn to do anything is never to learn to do an individual act; it is always to learn to do acts of a certain kind in a certain kind of situation, and this is to learn a principle.[1]

We learn to make moral judgements by being taught principles, or general rules, which we have seen are thought to resemble 'Avoid body sway when teeing off' in golf, or 'Depress clutch when changing gear' in driving. But this is confusing. For such principles are of value only to someone who already understands what 'body sway' or 'depressing the clutch' signify. If I want to teach a novice to change gear, I have first to explain what I mean by 'depressing the clutch'.

Now, if we suppose that a child learns to eschew lying by means of judgements like 'Lying is wrong', *and* we think of these as general rules or principles, we presuppose that the child already knows what lying is. Further, he must understand lying purely factually, for he has not yet learned to attach any moral significance to it. On Hare's account, then, the ability to make moral judgements presupposes the ability to make purely factual judgements. We see the world factually and only then do we come to see it morally. It is easy to see why such accounts present philosophers with an apparent gap between facts and values.

[1] *The Language of Morals*, p. 60.

Facts and 'Pure' Facts

In this respect it is interesting to consider some of the remarks which Piaget makes in his *Moral Judgement of the Child*. Piaget found that small children, when asked what constitutes lying, tended to equate it with swearing or the use of indecent terms. Thus one child pointed out that 'A lie is words you mustn't say, naughty words',[1] another, when asked whether the word 'fool' was a lie, answered that it was,[2] and so on. Piaget comments:

> There seems therefore only one explanation; to tell a lie is to commit a moral fault by means of language. And using naughty words also constitutes a fault committed by means of language. So that for the little child . . . the two types of conduct are on the same plane. When he pronounces certain sentences that do not conform to the truth . . . he is astonished to find that they provoke the indignation of those around, and that he is reproached with them as with a fault. When he brings in certain expressive words from the street the same things happen. He concludes that there are things one may say and things one may not say, and he calls the latter 'lies'.[3]

Piaget's subjects were already acquainted with the social condemnation of lying, even though their understanding of what a lie involves was still confused. They did not learn to identify lies in a factual sense and then learn that lies are to be condemned. By the time that they were able to give a correct factual definition, their concept of lying was already invested with moral import.

Before we pursue this line of argument any further, it may be necessary to guard against a misunderstanding. And in order to do this we must distinguish firmly between two possible theses.

1. We saw earlier that Hare and Mrs. Foot adhere to the view that moral judgements are made on the basis of certain facts. My criticisms have been directed against one possible interpretation of this view. I have tried to show that these facts are not to be equated with purely neutral descriptions.

---

[1] *The Moral Judgement of the Child*, p. 137.
[2] Ibid.   [3] Ibid., pp. 138–9.

Moral Reasoning

2. Someone might, however, wish to maintain a far more radical, and I believe false, thesis. It might be argued that there are certain terms for which *no* factual equivalent can be given. This sort of manœuvre seems especially plausible in the case of concepts like lying, murder, or promise-keeping. After all, lying is not just 'saying what is false', but saying what is false in order to deceive; murder is not merely the taking of life (which might constitute an act of war or self-defence), but rather, as Melden has pointed out, 'the wilful and deliberate killing of another human being',[1] and to make a promise is surely just to put oneself under a moral obligation to do something. In none of these cases are purely factual descriptions given. Perhaps they could not be given. But, if so, does it not follow that there are certain moral judgements ('He lied', 'He promised', 'He committed murder') which could not, from their very nature, be founded on statements of fact.

It is important to realise that this *is* a far more radical thesis than my own. On my account the concept of, say, murder may indeed possess moral import. But it will do so only within a particular way of life. (Whether there is, as a matter of fact, any way of life in which it does not do so is a different matter.) On the other hand, if the above accounts were correct, then it would be inconceivable that it should not be so. We should not even be able to imagine a society for which murder was a matter of moral indifference, since to understand what murder involved would be to accept a moral attitude towards it.

To this Hare provides what seems to me a conclusive objection. In *Freedom and Reason* he points out that if there were a term for which no factual equivalent could be given, it would always be possible to use some other term or to invent a new one.[2] For example, it may be true that we cannot refer to a patient in a mental hospital as a 'madman' without committing ourselves to a certain attitude towards such people. This is why people with a more humane atti-

---

[1] *Rights and Right Conduct*, p. 61.
[2] See, for example, *Freedom and Reason*, p. 188.

tude have introduced terms like 'mentally ill'. Their aim is to substitute a morally neutral term, in this case a medical one, for a concept which has become invested with (unfavourable) moral import.

The more radical thesis, then, is false. It constitutes no objection to the account which we are considering. Fortunately we do not have to go so far in order to show that this account is misconceived. We can admit that it is possible to give a purely factual equivalent for any moral concept, admit that any moral judgement must ultimately rest on factual considerations, and yet deny that these considerations have a purely factual status within a morality.

Let us imagine someone who, like Camus' 'Outsider', is devoid of any moral sense, but who is in all other respects the same as the rest of mankind. Hare's point can now be expressed by saying that such a man might possess factual equivalents for all those concepts which, in our society, carry moral import. He might understand what murder, suicide and lying involve, even though for him these concepts would have no moral significance.

I do not think that such a situation is in any way inconceivable. We can quite easily imagine the sorts of things which such a man would say and do. He would, for instance, distinguish murder and accidental death or killing in self-defence, otherwise we should not say that he possessed our concept of murder. But for him the distinction would be without moral significance. He would not condemn murderers, nor would he feel remorse if he himself murdered another. Thus Camus' 'Outsider', when he is arrested for murder, remarks, 'I wasn't conscious of any sin; all I knew was that I'd been guilty of a criminal offence.'[1]

If this were all Hare were maintaining, then it would be quite unobjectionable. Unfortunately he goes further than this. He wishes to say not merely that the facts may be without moral import, as they are for Meursault, but that they always are without moral import. For Meursault the fact that he has murdered a man has no moral significance.

[1] *The Outsider*, p. 116.

Hare believes that in so far as this is a factual matter, it has no moral significance for the rest of us.

Prima facie, this contention seems absurd. If I were to meet someone like Meursault, I should expect to disagree with him about murder. True, the disagreement would not be an empirical one. There would be no facts which he would assert and which I should deny. But our attitudes towards murder would be different. I should condemn murderers, whereas our 'Outsider' would neither praise nor blame them.

Hare's answer is that, although in both cases the fact of murder (*qua* fact) is neutral, there is a difference in that the members of my society have adopted a moral position towards murder, whereas Meursault has neither made nor adopted any such decision. Of course, Hare realises that not all of a man's values are of his own making. His point is simply that the origin of, say, the prohibition on murder can only be explained in terms of some individual's decision. If I did not myself decide that murder is wrong, then I must have merely adopted someone else's decision. Whatever is praised or condemned in my society, someone at some time must have asked themselves whether these things were right or wrong.

My difficulty is that I do not know what meaning this question could have for someone for whom nothing had any moral significance. How would they answer it? What considerations would they appeal to in reaching a decision? Clearly for them there could be *no* such considerations. For suppose that they were to say that, e.g., murder was wrong because it causes suffering to those involved (not that I think that this would be very plausible). In this case there would be at least one fact – suffering – which had moral significance for them, one place where the distinction between factual and moral considerations could not be drawn. But if, as Hare maintains, no facts had any moral significance, then there would be no criteria for deciding whether anything was good or bad, and the question would have no sense.

It is worth emphasising that this difficulty in Hare's

account is a logical one. The whole idea of a man making moral judgements on the basis of morally neutral facts is incoherent. My earlier remarks about the way in which children learn to use terms like 'greed' or 'suicide' may have given the impression that I was indicating a mere matter of psychological fact. Granted, it might be said, that Hare's account of moral development is faulty; granted that there are certain concepts which have both factual and moral significance for a child; is it not just a contingent matter that this is so, rather than a logical necessity?

In one sense this is true. We can, if we wish, call it a contingent matter that, for instance, a Catholic child should be brought up to attach a moral significance to suicide. We should then mean that if it had been brought up in a different way of life, this fact might have had a different significance, or perhaps no significance at all. This is quite consistent with my thesis. On the other hand, to say that there must be some facts which have a moral significance for a man, if he is to make moral judgements, is a statement of logical necessity. For it is only because there are certain things which do have moral significance for him, only because he is a member of a morality in which men value certain things, that he has any grounds on which to base moral judgements.

For this reason, Hare's account is misconceived. He asks us to imagine a situation in which nothing has moral import, in which all the facts are pure facts, and then to explain how it is that we come to make moral judgements. To this question there is no answer. If nothing has any moral worth, then there is nothing on which to found a moral judgement, no basis for deciding what is good or bad. Once we admit that within a moral code certain things do have moral worth for a man, this difficulty disappears. But it now becomes impossible to draw a rigid distinction between facts and values here. Within a particular viewpoint the distinction is meaningless. Outside *any* viewpoint it is a complete dichotomy.

We are now, I think, in a position to consider what might

seem a conclusive objection to my account. I have been maintaining that within a moral code there can be no gap between factual and moral judgements. For instance, I have tried to show that we cannot understand the significance which suicide has within a Catholic morality unless we realise that in this context to say that a man has committed suicide *is* to say that he has sinned.

But, it might be asked, how can this be maintained? Catholics regard suicide as the supreme sin, but surely it still makes sense to ask whether suicide is wrong. And if this question is intelligible, how can 'X committed suicide' mean 'X did wrong', even for a Catholic?

My answer to this well-known objection should by now be clear. Within the Catholic morality the question 'Is suicide wrong?' is redundant. The objection seems well-founded only because it fails to specify the context in which the question would be intelligible. Nor can we remove the difficulty by saying that the question arises in 'ordinary language' or in 'the ordinary use of the word "suicide" '. Ordinary men talk about suicide in many different ways, and what it makes sense for them to say depends on the morality to which they belong. To talk about the 'ordinary' uses of moral terms only conceals this diversity.

Certainly I should not wish to deny that within some ways of life the question 'Is suicide wrong?' can have a sense. Here there will be the possibility of considerations for and against suicide, and the way in which the agent answers will depend on which of these considerations he regards as the more important. Nor do I deny that the question might arise for a particular Catholic. It does so for Rose in Greene's *Brighton Rock*. Rose's husband has persuaded her to join him in a suicide pact, but when he hands her the weapon with which she is to kill herself, she finds herself in a dilemma:

> If it was a guardian angel speaking to her now, he spoke like a devil – he tempted her to virtue like a sin. To throw away the gun was a betrayal; it would be an act of cowardice; it would mean that she chose never to see him again for ever. Moral maxims dressed up

in pedantic, priestly tones remembered from old sermons, instructions, confessions – 'You can plead for him at the throne of Grace' – came to her like unconvincing insinuations. The evil act was the honest, the bold and the faithful – it was only lack of courage, it seemed to her, that spoke so virtuously.[1]

Although Rose feels the strength of her Catholic upbringing, doubt has begun to creep in. It should not surprise us that this is possible. For a morality is not like an exclusive club. There will be traffic between those who belong to it, and those outside it. Throughout her life Rose will probably have come into contact with those who do not share her viewpoint. Considerations which weigh with them will come to weigh with her. And this may cause conflict and doubt. Rose feels that it would be wrong to commit suicide. But she also feels that it would be disloyal to her husband, a 'betrayal', not to commit suicide. But the doubt comes from outside the Catholic morality. The considerations which give sense to the question 'Is suicide wrong?' are not Catholic considerations. *Within* the Catholic morality they do not count as reasons for committing suicide. They are simply a temptation.

[1] *Brighton Rock*, p. 244.

9
The Possibility of Conflicting Values

In the Introduction to this essay, I noted one important difference between processes of moral justification and the sort of justification appropriate to an empirical or scientific judgement, a difference which I there expressed by saying that a moral argument is liable to break down in a way that empirical or scientific arguments cannot.[1] When a man makes a factual assertion, although he may not expect that everyone will agree with him, he is justified in assuming that any disagreement which arises can, in principle, be resolved. When, on the other hand, he makes a moral judgement, it would be foolhardy to make any such assumption. For there often seem to be moral disputes where nothing that either party says will bring about agreement.

In the next two chapters I intend to return to these kinds of question, in order to see whether the account of moral reasoning which I have been advocating will shed any light on them. This chapter I shall devote to a consideration of those features of moral disagreements (and later, moral problems) which tend to make them more intractable than other sorts of disputes and problems. In this way I hope to show what is wrong with the sort of approach advocated by Mrs. Foot. In the following chapter I shall consider the extent to which agreement is necessary within the sphere

[1] See p. x.

The Possibility of Conflicting Values

of morality, if moral discourse is to be possible, and in this way indicate my reasons for rejecting Hare's account. I shall conclude by trying to summarise the ways in which my account alone can explain both the agreement and the disagreement which characterise moral discourse.

Perhaps the best way in which to see why moral arguments may reach deadlock is to consider why this does *not* happen in many other types of argument. Why, for example, is it that empirical or scientific disagreements always seem capable in principle of being resolved? And which characteristics of such disputes can we point to in order to account for this difference?

Suppose, for instance, that two electricians are mending a wireless, and that they disagree over whether there is a current running through a part of the circuit. X says, 'That length of wire is live'. Y denies this. Here we have a fairly typical empirical dispute and there is an *accepted* procedure by which it may be resolved. If, for example, the wire gives an electric shock when touched, lights an electric bulb inserted in the circuit, or gives an ammeter-reading, then X is right. If not, then Y is right. Of course, X and Y disagree over what the facts of the case *are*. X believes that the wire will give an ammeter-reading. Y does not. What they do not disagree over is the relevance, the significance of the facts.

The reason why this is so is that the relevance of the facts is itself determined by the meaning of the terms in which the dispute is couched. Part of what X means when he says that the wire is live is that it will give a shock if touched with the unprotected hand. Part of what Y means when he denies this is that a bulb inserted in the circuit will not light up.

This becomes clear if we ask ourselves how we teach a child the meaning of such statements. Generally we do so by indicating the situations in which they can be used correctly. We point out that if a wire gives a tingling sensation or lights a bulb, then it is live; if it does none of these things, we explain that it contains no current. That is, we show the child the criteria by which the truth or falsity of the statement is established. And we test his understanding in the same way. We ask for criteria for saying that the wire is electrified. And if he says that a wire is live simply because, e.g., it has red insulation, we say that he has misunderstood the meaning of 'live'.

Now what this shows is that where both parties to an empirical dispute agree on the meaning of the terms involved, there can be no dispute over the criteria which are relevant to its solution. This is why we can say that an empirical dispute must be capable of being solved. Of course, this does not mean that the solution will always be easy to find. Nor even that in practice it will be possible to find it. What it means is that it does not make sense to say 'This dispute has no solution'.

Now it seems to me that when we consider moral disagreements the temptation is that of assimilating them to empirical disagreements. Obsessed with an empirical model, philosophers have wanted to deny the difference between the two types of dispute. In particular, they have wanted to say that moral disputes (like empirical disputes) must be capable of solution. What I want to maintain is that it makes no sense at all to say this, as I shall try to show by means of a concrete example.

Consider the question whether scientists should carry out experiments on live animals in the interests of research, and in particular whether *vivisection* is morally justified as a part of scientific method. There are many possible attitudes here. But for our present purpose we need indicate only two conflicting viewpoints.

1. Some people would say that scientific research must continue even where it involves the suffering and death of animals. Precisely what this position amounts to, and the arguments which are relevant to it, will of course depend on the scientist's view of his work. He may, for instance, regard science merely as a technique for meeting the demands of society (or rather of certain dominant social groups). Here vivisection becomes just a means to an end, although since the end is a moral one, we can nevertheless say that a moral

The Possibility of Conflicting Values

justification is being offered. On the other hand, the scientist *may* see vivisection as one aspect of something which has a value in itself, namely free enquiry, or the scientific way of life. And it is this latter position with which I wish to concern myself.

2. On the other hand, many people would wish to disagree with the scientist's position. 'Regardless of its value to science', they might argue, 'vivisection is an evil practice.' Of course, such a person does not need to deny the importance which the scientist attaches to his work. They merely feel that it is more important that living creatures should not suffer.

Now, in what respects does this sort of disagreement differ from empirical disagreement? Primarily, I think, in that it no longer makes sense to talk of an 'accepted procedure for settling the dispute', or of 'common evidence'. Certainly in one sense the scientist and the anti-vivisectionist may agree over the facts. For example, neither may wish to deny that vivisection causes suffering, or that it is a valuable aid to research. These are both facts on which they are agreed. But to point to them is unlikely to bring about moral agreement. For, as we have seen, the disagreement arose in the first place because, for the scientist, his work was of greater importance than any suffering (perhaps even personal suffering) which it might involve, whereas, for the anti-vivisectionist, the suffering was the overriding consideration.

Of course, those who oppose vivisection are not normally content to say that it causes suffering or pain. They maintain that the suffering is 'wanton', 'gratuitous', or 'pointless', and that it is something for which no justification can be given. Unfortunately, this consideration is no longer a purely factual one. For whether or not suffering is pointless, is not something which can be established in independence of a man's moral position. The anti-vivisectionist may believe it to be so. But the scientist holds that the value of his researches gives a point to any suffering which they may entail.

Moral Reasoning

If there were any 'common evidence' in terms of which conflicting viewpoints could be reconciled, it would be because, in moral disputes as in empirical disputes, the relevance of this evidence was determined by the meaning of the terms involved. Many philosophers have tried to maintain that this is indeed so. Thus Bentham says:

> Of an action that is conformable to the principle of utility one may always say either that it is one that ought to be done, or at least that it is not one that ought not to be done. One may say also, that it is right it should be done; at least that it is not wrong it should be done: that it is a right action; at least that it is not a wrong action. When thus interpreted the words 'ought', and 'right' and 'wrong', and others of that stamp, have a meaning, when otherwise they have none.[1]

But Bentham's point rests on a fundamental misconception. As we have already seen, in moral arguments whatever significance the facts may have is determined, not by the meanings of the terms involved in the dispute, but by the moral convictions of the disputants, that is, by the moralities to which they belong. To suppose that, for example, the disagreement between the scientist and the anti-vivisectionist could be settled by an appeal to the 'facts' is to assume that the facts possess the same moral significance for both of them. But, if this were so, the disagreement could hardly have arisen. In order to account for the dispute, we have to realise that the scientist has been brought up in an environment where great importance is attached to the scientific way of life. His views have, at least partly, been formed by discussions with people who use terms like 'unscientific' to express disapproval. The anti-vivisectionist by contrast has been influenced by his contact with those who oppose suffering, but who do not necessarily attach any overriding importance to the aims and purposes of scientists. Consequently, when these ways of life come into conflict, there is no neutral standard, no 'common evidence', by which the dispute can be resolved. The standards of relevance are

[1] *Introduction to the Principles of Morals and Legislation*, p. 4.

The Possibility of Conflicting Values

themselves in dispute. Because of this, it does not make sense to say that there must be a solution to the dispute.

Perhaps I should emphasise that this is a logical point and not an empirical one. For philosophers like Mrs. Foot, who wish to deny the 'breakdown view', often confuse the two. In 'Moral Arguments' for instance, we are told that:

> Looked at in one way, the assertion that moral arguments 'may always break down' appears to make a large claim. What is meant is that they may break down in a way in which other arguments may not. . . . Now the question is: how can we assert that any disagreement about right and wrong may end like this? How do we know, without consulting the details of each argument, that there is always an impregnable position both for the man who says that x is right, or good, or what he ought to do, and for the man who denies it?[1]

Mrs. Foot talks as though the issue between those who maintain the breakdown view and those who deny it were an empirical one. The assertion that moral arguments may always break down is said to be a 'large claim', a generalisation about the outcome of any moral argument. And to this she rightly objects that no one can know *what* the outcome will be. We have to consider the details of each argument.

But the position which Mrs. Foot is attacking is not one which I should care to defend. What I have been trying to show is that it does not make sense to say of a moral argument that it *must* have a solution. Nor, of course, does it make sense to say that it must have *no* solution. But neither of these statements says anything about the outcome of any disagreement about right and wrong. On the contrary, what they show is that we *cannot* say anything *a priori* about this outcome.

Indeed, what is interesting about the passage in question is that it contradicts, not my own views, but those of Mrs. Foot. Mrs. Foot is maintaining that we cannot make *a priori* judgements about moral disputes; that we cannot say, without consulting the details, whether any dispute will or will not be solved. Unfortunately, this emphasises

[1] 'Moral Arguments', p. 502.

just those differences between empirical and moral disagreement which she is concerned to deny. For the point is that we *can* say *a priori* how an empirical dispute will turn out. We do not need to consider the details of, e.g., the argument between the two electricians to know that one of them is wrong, and that there must be some solution to their disagreement. It is precisely in this respect that empirical disagreement differs from moral disagreement.

Because it ignores such differences then, the approach championed by Mrs. Foot is unable to account for moral disputes. But what of moral problems? Do they present similar difficulties, or are they more amenable to Mrs. Foot's account?

The first thing to note is that there is a close analogy between moral disagreement and personal moral perplexity; an analogy which might be expressed by saying that moral disputes occur when two or more people bring different considerations to bear on the same situation, moral problems when there is a conflict between the considerations which the same man regards as relevant to a given situation. Shakespeare's *Measure for Measure* provides a good example of the sort of problem with which I am concerned. Angelo, an abstinent and self-righteous deputy of the Duke of Vienna, is entrusted by him with the government of the city, and immediately condemns to death one of his subjects, Claudio, for the crime of lechery. When Isabella, Claudio's sister and a novice of the 'votarists of Saint Clare',[1] goes to plead for her brother's life, Angelo succumbs to the vice which he has judged so harshly in others and offers her two alternatives. Either Claudio will be executed for his crime, or Angelo can use his authority to see that he is set free. But he will do so only if Isabella agrees to sleep with him.

In order to understand Isabella's problem we have to consider the different social groups to which she belongs, in particular, the religious movement of which she is a member, and the institution of the family. As a nun, Isabella is committed to a life of chastity. But she also

[1] *Measure for Measure*, I, iv, 5.

The Possibility of Conflicting Values

belongs to a family, and this involvement brings with it duties and obligations of a different sort. The tragedy is that in the circumstances in which she finds herself, the duties arising from her participation in these different ways of life conflict. As a nun, she must preserve her virtue. As a sister, she must do what is in her power to save her brother's life. But to do the one will prevent her doing the other.

In a society of any complexity such problems are bound to arise, for there will be numerous social groups all giving rise to different standards of right and wrong conduct. We may think, for instance, of the duties and obligations stemming from membership of a trade union, of codes of military or medical ethics, of one's obligation to the family, or to a religious movement, of a citizen's duty to obey the laws of his country, and so on. And in many cases there will be the possibility of moral conflict for the man or woman who belongs to one or more of these groups. It is difficult even to imagine a society from which such conflicts would be absent. As Simone Weil says:

> We cannot even be sure that the idea of an order in which all obligations would be compatible with one another isn't itself a fiction. When duty descends to the level of facts, so many independent relationships are brought into play that incompatibility seems far more likely than compatibility.[1]

Certainly, in a primitive society, the possible sources of incompatibility may be limited. Much moral perplexity arises from the demands which religion or profession make upon a man. And I suppose that we can imagine a society from which these sorts of institution are absent. But even in a society where a man's only moral obligations are those imposed by the family, it is clear that he may still face conflicts. Obligations to his mother may clash with those to his wife, and so on.

For this reason I find some of Karl Popper's remarks in *The Open Society* unconvincing. Popper holds that in what he calls a 'closed society' (or 'tribal way of life')

[1] *The Need for Roots*, p. 10.

Moral Reasoning

taboos rigidly dominate all aspects of life. They do not leave loopholes. There are few problems in this form of life and nothing really equivalent to moral problems.[1]

A participant in such a way of life 'will rarely find himself in the position of doubting how he ought to act. The right way is always determined.'[2]

One wonders how Popper can say that such a society will never give rise to anything 'equivalent to a moral problem'. Surely one could say this only if one knew what situations the members of the society were going to encounter during their lives. Perhaps it would be possible to say that a man would never be the subject of conflicting obligations if he recognised only *one* obligation – say, the obligation not to commit murder. But, even if this is a logical possibility (which I am not sure that it is), it is clear that Popper is not thinking of such a situation.

Moral problems, then, are rooted in the sort of life which a man leads, in the moralities to which he belongs. This is an important difference between moral problems and the kind of empirical problems which we have been considering. A problem such as that which faced our electricians is not a part of the enquiry within which it arises, but an obstacle to it. True, such problems may also arise within any way of life. Man's knowledge is limited, and though there is a right answer to every (empirical) problem, we do not always know the answer. But Isabella's problem does not arise because her knowledge is limited, because there is a right answer to her difficulty of which she is unaware. Her problem is that she feels both of the alternatives open to her to be wrong. Whether she gives herself to Angelo or betrays her brother, she will feel remorse for what she has done. This is why we feel such problems to be in some way tragic.

Many philosophers would, however, wish to deny my account of the differences. They want to maintain that *any* problem must be capable of solution, and that moral prob-

[1] *The Open Society*, vol. I, p. 172. [2] Ibid.

The Possibility of Conflicting Values

lems are no exception. Renford Bambrough, for instance, says:

> the complexity and difficulty of moral choice ... is no greater than the complexity and difficulty which we face in many non-moral enquiries ...

for example:

> history, sociology, textual criticism, meteorology, cosmology, molecular biology.[1]

The list of subjects which Bambrough gives is fairly diverse, and I do not think that they could all be said to be examples of purely empirical studies. History, for example, is not just concerned to discover facts about the past, but also involves the evaluation of these facts. To this extent what Bambrough says begs the question. On the other hand, in so far as such enquiries are simply concerned with matters of fact (as are molecular biology and meteorology), then, although no one would deny that they may give rise to problems of overwhelming complexity, I want to say that they are not of the same *kind* of complexity as moral problems.

An historian may wish to establish whether or not Columbus discovered America, and in this case the problem which he sets himself is a purely empirical one, to be solved by amassing information about the explorer's life, consulting historical authorities, and so on. No doubt this will be a complicated task. But it lacks one sort of complexity which characterises the problems of morality. For our historian can at least assume that there will be general agreement over the nature of his problem. Other historians may disagree with his conclusions. But they will not disagree over the nature of the difficulties which he faces. These are the same for anyone who concerns himself with this topic. This is why, for instance, specialists in these fields may work together to solve some of their problems.[2]

[1] 'Unanswerable Questions', p. 157.
[2] Although not the most important of their problems, for, as I have said, these are problems of evaluation and interpretation.

With a moral problem, however, it is quite different. The problem in *Measure for Measure*, for example, is not the same for everyone, but is essentially one which Isabella has to solve for herself. Nor do I mean this in the trivial sense that we are not all called upon to make a choice between chastity and the life of someone dear to us, although of course this is true. Rather, I am saying that the sort of external situation which Isabella faces might well not constitute a problem for someone else.

Isabella's perplexity stems from the importance which she attaches both to her chastity and to her brother's life. For someone who attached a different importance to these things, who felt perhaps that one's religious obligations should come before all else, the problem might be quite different. For them the situation would give rise to no conflicting obligations; rather it would be a straightforward choice between doing what is right and succumbing to temptation. Again, Isabella's brother, Claudio, sees the problem in yet another way:

> Sweet sister, let me live.
> What sin you do to save a brother's life,
> Nature dispenses with the deed so far
> That it becomes a virtue.[1]

It would not make sense to ask which of these interpretations accords with the facts. In the sense in which it is intelligible to speak of 'the correct interpretation' of an historical problem, there can be no correct interpretation of Isabella's problem, for we cannot make any general distinction between how it presents itself to different people, to Claudio or Isabella, and how it really is, independently of anyone's moral beliefs. In this it is quite different from, for instance, the problem of whether Columbus discovered America. For suppose that the historian in our example were to begin his enquiry with a consideration of Magna Carta. Here we should be quite justified in saying that he had simply misunderstood the nature of the problem facing him, for the

[1] Shakespeare, op. cit., III, i, 130-3.

The Possibility of Conflicting Values

correct interpretation of an historical problem is independent of any individual's beliefs. Whatever striking conclusions he might reach, we should feel that they rested on a mistake. But it would not make sense to speak in this way of Isabella's problem. This depends on the way in which *she* sees the issues confronting her. Certainly it does not follow that what is to count as a moral problem is something that we can choose. To say this would be to ignore the way in which moral perplexity is forced on us by the social groups to which we belong. My point is simply that whether or not something counts as a moral problem will depend on one's moral viewpoint.

It follows that whether or not something counts as a solution of a man's problem will also depend on his moral viewpoint, a point which has been consistently ignored by those philosophers who, like Bentham or Mrs. Foot, have wanted to maintain that moral problems must have a solution valid for all. Whether (as in the case of Mrs. Foot) this solution has been sought in the facts of good and harm, or (as with Bentham) in the happiness of the greatest number, it has always been tacitly assumed that there is one correct account of a moral problem, of which all other accounts are misinterpretations. Only on this assumption does it make sense to speak of a solution which everyone will accept.

My point is that a problem like that which Isabella faces cannot be solved in the way that a problem in history can, that is by means of some accepted procedure. If it is solved at all, then this will be because Isabella comes to see that the obligations to her family and religion are not of equal importance, that there are certain considerations which have an overriding claim on her. But it is just a confusion to speak of an agreed procedure by which someone may 'come to see' this. As it happens, Isabella realises that her first obligation is to her religion:

> Then, Isabel, live chaste, and, brother, die:
> More than our brother is our chastity.[1]

[1] Shakespeare, op. cit., II, iv, 185–6.

This may not be the solution which another person would accept. They may feel perhaps that the prospect of Claudio's death should be the overriding consideration here. For them the reference to physical harm decides the matter. But to assume that such considerations will always be decisive is just a misunderstanding. Isabella realises that her brother will suffer if she does not agree to Angelo's proposal. But this does not solve her difficulties. It creates them. Her problem is that she cannot decide whether she ought to do what will prevent Claudio suffering. And this is not a question which can be answered by reference to 'the facts of good and harm'. It is not necessarily a question to which there is any answer at all.

What I have tried to show in this chapter, then, is that we cannot say of a moral dispute (or a moral problem) that it must be solved. To suppose that we can is to ignore those characteristics of moral arguments which distinguish them from empirical arguments. Nevertheless, I have also tried to show that I am not thereby committed to the obviously false assertion that no moral dispute is ever capable of solution. To deny that a solution *must* be found is not to say that it *will not* be found, only that it *need not*.

And, of course, moral disputes may be solved in a variety of ways. It may, for instance, be that one party to the dispute offers reasons which the other finds convincing. Or perhaps one of them is forced to realise that adherence to certain of his moral convictions will have unacceptable consequences – consequences to which he has hitherto been blind. It may even be that, although neither party brings forward any further consideration at all, one of them simply comes to see that his opponent is right. I should not want to deny that any of these alternatives is possible. All I wish to maintain is that no one can say in advance that the dispute must be solved in any of these ways.

Unfortunately, my account of moral disagreement may well be felt to be open to a further objection. Admittedly, nothing that I have said precludes the possibility that men of different moral viewpoints will resolve their differences.

The Possibility of Conflicting Values

Nevertheless, it may be thought to rule out the possibility of any *rational* solution. If, so the argument runs, there is no established procedure by which such a dispute can be solved, then surely, even where agreement is reached, the 'solution' cannot be regarded as anything but arbitrary.

What is to be noted is that this sort of objection rests on the assumption that any dispute which cannot be settled by means of some established procedure, can be settled only in arbitrary manner. This assumption, common among empiricist philosophers, is particularly evident in the writings of Bentham. The argument of chapter 1 of the *Principles*, for example, clearly presupposes that the following are exhaustive alternatives: either a man founds his judgements, arguments and convictions on some accepted principle (and, of course, Bentham believes that the only such principle is that of utility), or he founds them on 'the mere averment of his own unfounded sentiment; that is, what in another person he might be apt to call caprice'. Once again, however, I should want to maintain that this will seem plausible only to someone who accepts as their paradigm an empirical model of disagreement. Suppose that the electricians in our earlier example had decided to ask for advice from an expert. And suppose that, instead of explaining to them the use of an ammeter, how to wire a bulb into a circuit, and so on, our expert had simply tossed a coin. Here we should clearly protest that this is an arbitrary way of deciding the matter. And the reason why this is so, is that what we expect from our expert is a technique. In the field of electrical engineering there are accepted procedures for settling disputes, and to ignore these *is* to act in an arbitrary manner. This is what 'arbitrary' means here.

But, as we have seen, moral disputes cannot be solved in this sort of way. Indeed where, as in the argument between the scientist and the anti-vivisectionist, disagreement is really deep-rooted, it is unlikely that it will be solved by any reasons which either party brings forward. This is what I meant when I said that in such a case moral breakdown is

[1] *An Introduction to the Principles of Morals and Legislation*, p. 6.

Moral Reasoning

likely. Nevertheless, it is still possible that the dispute will be solved, if one of the disputants changes his views. It may, for instance, be that the scientist will just realise that he is wrong to attach an overriding importance to the pursuit of his researches; he may come to see that there are other and more important considerations to which he has hitherto been blind. And so he may find that he now agrees with his opponent in condemning vivisection.

Does it follow that the dispute between them has been settled in a merely arbitrary fashion? Surely this would make sense only if we had some right to suppose that it might be solved in a different way. If a judge were to decide cases in court on the basis of whether the defendant *looked* honest, we should regard his decisions as arbitrary. There is a complex system of principles for settling legal issues, and we expect judges to make use of it. But in morality there is no comparable procedure. To condemn the solution of a moral dispute as arbitrary because of this, is like condemning the solution of a mathematical problem as arbitrary because it is not reached by empirical observation. This is *not* what 'arbitrary' means here.

Of course, we do sometimes refer to a man's moral decisions as arbitrary, not because he has failed to make use of some technique in reaching them, but because we feel that he has acted insincerely in some way. I might say that the change in our scientist's views was arbitrary, and then I should mean that his heart was not in it. 'Deep down', I might say, 'he does not really believe that vivisection is wrong. What he says does not carry conviction.' But of course there are also cases where we should not say this. When Prince Nekhludov in Tolstoi's *Resurrection* says:

> Everything was clear. It was clear that everything considered important and good was insignificant and repulsive[1]

we realise that this is not just an arbitrary decision. Nekhludov's friends and relations may regard the change which has come over him as a mere whim. But it is clear

[1] *Resurrection*, p. 338.

The Possibility of Conflicting Values

that they are wrong. Nekhludov solves the problems which have been tormenting him, when he realises that he has ignored those things in life which are of real importance. This is nothing like tossing a coin. I may toss a coin where I do not care about the alternatives, or where I must reach a decision quickly. But it does not help me to solve my problems. It is a way of acting without having to solve a problem. But for Nekhludov, what he says has the air of a discovery. For though he finds out no new facts about the world, he does come to see that one way of living is contemptible, and that another is the only one possible for him:

> He wished to forget all this, not to see it, but he could no longer help seeing it. Though he could not see the source of the light which revealed it to him any more than he could see the source of the light which lay over St. Petersburg; and though the light appeared to him dull, dismal and unnatural, yet he could not help seeing what it revealed, and he felt both joyful and anxious.[1]

To refer to this change as arbitrary, simply because there is no way in which it could have been predicted (or by which Nekhludov could have predicted it), is to impose a false criterion of arbitrariness, a criterion according to which no decision within morality could be anything but arbitrary. To say that Nekhludov's answer to his problems is not really a solution, is to ignore the fact that this is what we call a solution here.

[1] *Resurrection*, p. 339.

10
Agreement and Moral Communication

In the last chapter I tried to sum up some of the differences between moral and empirical disagreements which we have noted in this essay; in particular, I emphasised that in moral disputes there is no procedure by which general agreement can be ensured. However, it has also been one of my central contentions that it is a mistake to suppose that morality is therefore just a matter of individual choice, and that it is a merely contingent fact that men ever find themselves in agreement over moral issues.

In saying this, I am, of course, disagreeing with a long philosophical tradition according to which there is either one agreed moral standard which all men accept, or, as Bentham expressed it, 'as many different standards of right and wrong as there are men'.[1] A remark by Miss Ruby Meager provides a good illustration of how this tradition survives in contemporary philosophy:

> It must be obvious that the notion of a common factor in what we all, as human beings, must value, is a mistaken one, since ultimately what we all . . . value, is private to ourselves.[2]

What I have argued in the preceding chapters is that *both* of these alternatives may be consistently rejected. They may be

[1] Bentham, *Introduction to the Principles of Morals and Legislation*, p. 6.
[2] 'The Impossibility of a Common Factor . . .', p. 3.

rejected, simply because, although there *must* be agreement in what men regard as right and wrong if moral discourse is to be possible, the agreement in question is of a different kind from that which characterises empirical spheres.

The need for agreement in any type of discourse is well stated by Wittgenstein at *Philosophical Investigations*, 242:

> If language is to be a means of communication there must be agreement, not only in definitions, but also (queer as this may sound) in judgements.[1]

Wittgenstein's point is that an agreement in definitions logically presupposes an agreement in judgements. And in the case of empirical judgements, for instance colour-judgements, this is fairly clear. If men continually failed to agree whether an object were red or blue, if, to take an extreme case, there were as many standards of redness and blueness as there are men, then these words would become meaningless. For there would no longer be any distinction between applying them correctly and misapplying them. Nevertheless it is not often recognised that Wittgenstein's point applies not only to empirical terms, but to moral ones, and that if moral language is to be intelligible, there must be some agreement in what men regard as right and wrong.

In saying this, however, I do not think that I am committed to the sort of view that I attacked in the last chapter. For what I criticised there was not the idea that some agreement over moral issues is necessary, but rather the *sort* of agreement which some writers hold to be a feature of moral discourse; more precisely, I criticised the view that there is some kind of accepted technique by which *universal* moral agreement can be obtained. My own thesis is quite different. I have tried to show that it is *within a particular moral code* that we find the framework of agreement. For instance, we have seen that within a Catholic morality men agree in the significance which they attach to considerations like suicide and adultery, and it is from such considerations that their

[1] *Philosophical Investigations*, p. 88e.

use of the terms 'right' and 'wrong' draws its meaning. In saying this, I am of course rejecting Mrs. Foot's account, or any account according to which these terms have the same meaning for all of us. But I am also denying that their meaning is dependent on individual choice or decision. And this is what Hare maintains.

Unfortunately, were I to leave the matter there, it might well be thought that I had ignored much of Hare's account which is both true and important. For though it may be admitted that *The Language of Morals* and *Freedom and Reason* over-emphasise the importance of individual moral decisions, someone may nevertheless wish to say that my own account attaches too great an importance to the social aspects of morality. In particular, it may be suggested that, by anchoring the meaning of moral terms within a moral code, I have opened myself to the charge of conventionalism.

This objection is particularly relevant to my argument in chapter 7, where I maintained, in opposition to Hare, that the values which a child learns do not depend on his (or anyone else's) choices, but upon the way of life in which he is brought up. For this will probably be taken to imply that moral training is simply a process of teaching someone to act in the same way as others in his society. And this is certainly a confusion, for we expect those who have been brought up to know the difference between right and wrong, to be capable of more than socially conditioned responses to a situation. We assume, for example, that they will be able to make decisions and solve problems. And it is this aspect of morality with which Hare's account is primarily concerned. My own, by stressing the importance of considering moral judgements within a social setting, may seem to involve the view that 'society' is the final arbiter of right and wrong, and thus to rule out the possibility of moral decision.

This criticism is a forceful one, particularly since it draws attention to a mistake made by many philosophers who have held views of morality similar to my own. Bradley, for instance, emphasised the importance of studying moral judgements within the context of a particular way of life. He saw that a child

> is not born into a desert, but into a living world, a whole which has a true individuality of its own, and into a system and order which it is difficult to look on as other than an organism.[1]

He recognised that the learning of moral values can rarely be separated from the learning of language itself. The child

> learns, or perhaps has already learned to speak, and here he appropriates the common heritage of his race, the tongue that he makes his own is his country's language, it is (or it should be) the same that others speak, it carries into his mind the ideas and sentiments of the race ... and stamps them there indelibly.[2]

Unfortunately, Bradley tended to assume that this committed him to a conventionalist view of morality. Thus he quotes with approval Hegel's remark:

> that in respect of morality, the saying of the wisest men of antiquity is the only one which is true, that to be moral is to live in accordance with the moral tradition of one's country.[3]

Morality, on this view, becomes simply a process of adjusting to the demands of a particular group (in Hegel's case, the state), and certainly, in so far as such an account is accepted, it becomes difficult to see what part individual decisions have to play. In order to avoid censure, the moral agent need only voice and act upon the moral judgements of those around him. Bradley himself goes on to say, 'What is moral in any particular case is seldom doubtful. Society pronounces beforehand.'[4]

The question which we have to consider, then, is this: Does an emphasis on the social aspect of morality commit one to a conventionalist viewpoint? As the above quotations show, Bradley felt the two to be connected. And although it is part of Hare's purpose in *The Language of Morals* to reject any conventionalist approach to moral issues, the way in

---

[1] *Ethical Studies*, p. 171.   [2] Ibid., p. 173.
[3] Ibid.   [4] Ibid., p. 197.

which he does so shows that he accepts the same assumption. For he holds that it is only by *basing* morality on personal decision that conventionalism can be avoided.

Nevertheless, it seems to me that this is a confusion, and in what follows I shall try to show that my own view and conventionalism are quite distinct.

The confusion involved is, I think, part of a larger misconception about the nature of language in general. Earlier we took note of Wittgenstein's observation that a framework of human agreement is a precondition of meaningful discourse. We said, for instance, that if there were no consistency in people's application of colour-terms, one man referring to post-boxes or fire-engines as 'red', another man describing them as 'blue' or 'green', then these terms could not be said to have any definite meaning. Now, Wittgenstein himself foresaw one possible misunderstanding to which his account might give rise. At *Philosophical Investigations*, 241, he says:

> 'So you are saying that human agreement decides what is true and what is false?' – It is what human beings *say* that is true and false, and they agree in the *language* they use. That is not agreement in opinions but in a form of life.[1]

Wittgenstein is concerned here to distinguish his own view from a quite different view, which holds that the truth or falsity of, say, a colour-judgement is determined by whether or not others would agree with it, that is, the view that 'This is red' means 'This is what others would call "red" '. The distinction is important, not only because of the obvious falsity of this sort of account, but also because it involves a misunderstanding of what is meant in the *Philosophical Investigations* by 'human agreement'. For it implies (*a*) that men observe what others call red, and base their judgements on their observation, and (*b*) that the truth or falsity of these judgements is determined by whether or not they accord with those of others.

---

[1] *Philosophical Investigations*, p. 88e. I am indebted to Mr. H. O. Mounce for pointing out to me the relevance for ethics of Wittgenstein's remarks here.

Agreement and Moral Communication

Now it is the kind of agreement to which this theory refers that Wittgenstein calls 'agreement in opinions', and what must be noticed is that both 'agreement in opinions' and the distinction between truth and falsity are to be found within language. Neither gives language its sense; on the contrary, it is only because I understand colour-words that it is possible for me to observe that people agree in their opinions, and again it is only because my own colour-judgements have a meaning that the possibility of their being true or false arises. By contrast, when Wittgenstein speaks of 'agreement', he is speaking of what gives language its sense. This is not something that we could notice within language; it is not a part of the practice of making colour-judgements for instance, but rather something which must be presupposed if this practice is to be possible at all. His point is that unless there were a framework of agreement in the application of colour-terms, 'agreement in a form of life' as he puts it, then colour-discourse would be meaningless. He is not making a statement about the meaning or content of colour-judgements, but about the linguistic context in which they are intelligible.

The distinction between content and linguistic context is a crucial one for philosophy, but, unless I am mistaken, it has been ignored in the objection to my own account that we are considering. For here, as in the previous case, we must carefully distinguish *two* theses. That which lies at the basis of this essay maintains that moral judgements have a meaning only within the context of a particular morality (using Wittgenstein's terminology, we might say that moral discourse presupposes 'agreement in a form of life'). It should not be confused with the conventionalist theory that moral judgements are judgements about what others in that morality praise or condemn, for here the reference is to another sort of agreement – agreement in opinions. And once again it is important to recognise that these are distinct *kinds* of thesis. The first concerns the linguistic context in which moral judgements are intelligible. The second is a false statement about their content. To confuse them is to fall into just the sort of misunderstanding which Wittgenstein wished to expose.

To clarify these and other points, let us consider in greater detail what is meant by saying of someone that he is a conventionalist, or that he has a 'merely conventional' attitude towards morality. Hare indicates the main characteristics of this attitude when he describes the conventionalist use of language as that in which 'the speaker is merely paying lip-service to a convention, by commending, or saying commendatory things about, an object just because everyone else does'.[1] The tendency to merely repeat the judgements of other men is not, of course, confined to morality. Tolstoi's Stepan Arkadyevitch in *Anna Karenina* is an example of how it may run throughout a man's outlook on life:

> Stepan Arkadyevitch always read a liberal paper. It was not extreme in its views, but advocated those principles held by the majority of people. In spite of the fact that he was not really interested in science, or art, or politics, he strongly adhered to the same views on all such subjects as the majority and this paper in particular advocated, and changed them only when the majority changed. Or rather, it might be said, he did not change them at all – they changed of themselves imperceptibly.[2]

A similar attitude is to be found in Anna's husband, Alexei. Tolstoi says of him that

> he considered it his duty to read anything that had made a stir in the world of art, although art was utterly contrary to his nature. . . . He loved to talk of Shakespeare, Raphael and Beethoven, the importance of the new schools of music and poetry, which he classed most accurately.[3]

What is common to both Stepan and Alexei is that neither attaches any real importance to the subjects which he studies. Certainly in one way, they understand these subjects. Alexei, for instance, has an accurate knowledge of art. Probably it would be difficult to criticise his opinions, and

[1] *The Language of Morals*, p. 125. [2] *Anna Karenina*, p. 7.
[3] Ibid., p. 109.

Agreement and Moral Communication

this might lead us to attach a certain value to what he says. But in another sense he does not understand art at all. One would never say of him that he had a *profound* artistic understanding, for though he makes all the judgements that a true connoisseur would make, and is aware of the significance which they may have for others, for him they have no personal significance. Indeed, it is only in a superficial sense that we can think of Alexei's own judgements as *aesthetic* judgements at all, for ultimately they are not based on aesthetic considerations. True, when he praises or condemns a work of art, he may support his opinions with reasons which a real lover of the arts would accept, but these are not his real reasons. He holds these opinions simply because others do so.

A similar attitude characterises Alexei's morality, for though he acts in accordance with the precepts of his society (except in so far as they include the demand for sincerity, of course), he has no more moral feeling than artistic feeling, and does so simply to keep up appearances. We see this in his attitude to Anna's adultery. His concern over her affair with Vronsky is not primarily a moral one; he condemns her actions mainly because he fears that they will provoke the censure of others and threaten his position in society. Anna herself recognises this:

> 'Nothing but ambition – a desire to get on, that is the only thing he cares about,' she thought. 'As to his high ideals, his passion for culture, religion, they are only means to success.'[1]

Like all conventionalists, Alexei is contemptible because of his lack of sincerity. He feigns the moral convictions which others really possess, and in this respect he is similar to the moral hypocrite whom we considered in chapter 3. Of course, hypocrisy is generally condemned in a way that conventionalism is not. For the hypocrite conceals morally vicious behaviour beneath a façade of virtue, whereas the conventionalist's behaviour may well be socially acceptable. Nevertheless, as Hare points out, his existence constitutes

[1] Tolstoi, op. cit., p. 201.

a danger to the moral life of a community.[1] For, if a morality is to endure, then, tautologically, men must care about moral issues. And the conventionalist does not care.

There may, at first sight, seem to be a close connection between conventionalism and the account of morality which I am advocating, for in both cases the judgements which an individual makes might be said to depend on the moral standards of his society. Thus, on the one hand, we have seen that the conventionalist merely echoes the moral judgements of other men; on the other, I have maintained that *no* man's moral judgements can be understood in independence of some way of life to which they belong. Nevertheless, I do not think that this shows my account to be inconsistent with any distinction between the conventionalist's views and those of the true moral agent, but only that this distinction cannot be founded on whether or not their respective views depend on a social context. Rather the distinction centres around the kind of dependence which is involved.

The relationship between the views of the conventionalist and those of the rest of society is in certain respects analogous to that between a forgery and an original work of art. Just as the way in which a forger paints a picture is determined by the work of another artist, so the moral attitudes of other men are central in deciding what the conventionalist's attitude towards right and wrong shall be. Thus when Alexei Karenin condemns his wife's adultery, there is a clear sense in which it is for him a merely contingent matter that adultery is wrong, contingent upon the fact that it is condemned by the society of which he is a member.

Certainly, the contingent nature of Alexei's convictions is not something which will necessarily be apparent to others. He will not, for instance, *say* that he condemns Anna's affair simply because others do; this is not a reason which he might give, for, as we have seen, his prime concern is to avoid social condemnation, and conventionalism is itself one

[1] Hare, *The Language of Morals*, p. 149.

Agreement and Moral Communication

of the things which society condemns. The reasons which he gives may be superficially indistinguishable from those which a truly moral person would give. Nevertheless, they are in a sense incomplete. For the fact that he makes them at all, the fact that he chooses to take part in the practice of making moral judgements cannot be explained without reference to the views of others. In one way it is quite unimportant to him that Anna has committed adultery. What is important is that she has acted in a way contrary to the prevailing opinions in her society, for whatever the attitude of 19th-century Russian nobility towards adultery, this would be Alexei's attitude.

With the morally sincere man, this is not so. For though he may make the same judgements as Alexei, and for the same reasons, there is a difference in the significance which they have for him. Both may condemn Anna's behaviour. But in the sense in which Alexei's condemnation is contingent, the truly moral person's is not. For him it is a *sufficient* reason for condemning Anna that she has committed adultery.

Another aspect of this distinction is emphasised by Kierkegaard in *Purity of Heart*, when he asks rhetorically:

> But, my listener, would you dare, as a father (and I feel confident that you have a lofty conception of the meaning of this name, a reasonable conception of the charge which it lays upon you), would you dare, as a father, say to your child as you send him out into the world, 'Go with your mind at ease, my child, pay attention to what the many approve and what the world rewards, for that is the Good, but what the world punishes, that is evil. It is no longer true as it used to be that the judgement of the masses is like foam on water – nonsense, though loudly proclaimed; blind, though sharply decisive; impossible to follow, because it changes more swiftly than a woman changes colour....' Surely, my listener, the speech need not ask you, for it rests assured in advance what your answer would be.[1]

Kierkegaard's point is that, for the morally sincere man, there is a distinction between 'What the world approves' and 'What is right'. True, he may not have such a contempt

[1] *Purity of Heart*, p. 82.

for worldly opinion as Kierkegaard. His views may, to a large extent, be those of 'the many'. Nevertheless, it must be at least conceivable that he should find himself called upon to say, 'Whatever others may think, I regard so-and-so as right (or wrong)'. He must recognise the possibility of drawing a distinction between his own judgements and the judgement of the world. For the conventionalist, no such distinction is possible.

The views of the truly moral person, then, do not depend on 'society' in the sense in which those of the conventionalist do. But it does not follow that there is no sense in which they may be said to do so. And it is here that confusion is liable to arise. For, in explaining the difference between conventionalism and true morality, we have been concerned with the significance which moral considerations may have for a man. It is on this level that the conventionalist's views *alone* may be said to presuppose a social context. But when I say that *anyone's* views depend on a social context, I am talking on a quite different level. For I am not concerned with the question 'What significance do moral considerations have for different people?' but with the question 'What does it mean to say (or "How is it possible") that something is a moral consideration?' And I have said that *this* question can only be answered when we realise that no one decides what is to be regarded as having moral significance. On the contrary, what does and does not count as a moral consideration is determined by the way of life to which an individual belongs. Outside some such way of life, there can be no connection between facts and values, no connection between the reasons we give and the judgements that we make. That is to say, there can be no such thing as a moral judgement.

In saying this, however, I am making a statement about the conditions under which any moral judgement can be meaningful. I am not making a statement about the content of any individual's moral judgements, and in particular I am not equating them with those of a particular type of individual, namely the conventionalist. My point is that whatever a man's convictions, they can be understood only in so far as they are founded on socially accepted standards. Otherwise they would not be moral convictions at all.

If we now turn to consider the part which decision plays in morality, it will, I think, become clear that far from excluding this element, it is my account, and not Hare's, which allows us to give a coherent explanation of it. In this it is fundamentally different from the sort of conventionalist theory offered by Bradley, which does to a large extent deny the need for individual decision. For certainly, in so far as someone thinks of morality as a matter of acting in conformity with the judgements of others, he is unlikely to be faced with the sort of moral difficulties which normally face moral agents. Hare puts this point into the mouth of a hypothetical subjectivist:

> But surely, when it comes to the point – when I have listened to what other people say, and given due weight to my own intuitions, the legacy of my upbringing – I have in the end to decide for myself what I ought to do. To deny this is to be a conventionalist. . . . If I refuse to make my own decisions, I am, in merely copying my fathers, showing myself a lesser man than they; for whereas they must have initiated, I shall be merely accepting.[1]

Hare sees that the making of decisions is a crucial aspect of moral development, and an aspect which the conventionalist ignores. But this in no way contradicts my assertion[2] that a child's fundamental moral standards cannot be regarded as the result of a decision. There I pointed out that, far from it being the case that we learn to identify types of action in purely factual terms and only then come to attach moral significance to them, within a morality the learning of facts and values goes side by side. Just as a child learns to refer to certain actions as lies, without his being called upon to choose *this* word, so he comes to condemn lying without having to decide whether lying is perhaps praiseworthy.

No doubt imitation plays an important part in this process. For much of his early life the child is required to do little

---

[1] *The Language of Morals*, p. 77.   [2] See chapter 8.

more than voice and reproduce the moral judgements of those around him, of his parents and teachers. When he does so, he is praised. When he acts in ways of which they disapprove, he is punished. But, as Hare says, there is more involved in moral development than this. Though we may teach a child a morality by getting him to imitate, *what* we teach him is not the ability to imitate. If this were all that he ever learned, then we should be unable to describe his conduct in many of the ways appropriate to a discussion of adult behaviour. We should never say of him that he possessed moral insight or understanding, for instance. He would simply have mastered a technique or a ritual.

The point is that no matter how extensive or explicit the moral instruction which someone is given as a child, there comes a stage at which he is called upon to deal with moral problems, with conflicting duties or obligations. As we saw in the last chapter, even within a very simple family morality, where children are brought up to consider first and foremost the needs and rights of those related to them, it is at least possible for conflicts between a man's duties to different members of the family to arise. When this happens what is called for is not imitation, not even a very complex or sophisticated form of imitation, but capacities of a quite different kind. The man must *decide* what his moral viewpoint commits him to in this situation, whether for example his first obligation is to his mother or to his wife. And whichever alternative he chooses, others who share the same viewpoint may nevertheless disagree with him. *He* may feel that, because he has taken her away from her own family, because she is now dependent on him, he must stand by his wife. Someone else, on the other hand, may object that the overriding consideration should be the wishes of those who have cared for him since childhood, namely his parents. Here disagreement is possible, even though neither party disputes the fundamental importance of the family.

What we must not lose sight of is that, although such decisions play an important part in a man's moral life, their very possibility is dependent upon his having learned to value certain things (in the above case, the interests of the family), without the necessity for decision. True, unless he were capable of making his own moral judgements (and not just accepting those of others), we should be disinclined to say that he understood what morality involved. But if someone were to suppose that such judgements were *all* that is involved in morality, then I could only repeat what I have been saying throughout this essay, that unless a man had been brought up in a way of life in which certain considerations were of moral importance, then he would have no basis on which to make such judgements. A. E. Murphy (*The Theory of Practical Reason*) expresses this point well when he says that 'the point of moral training is to supply a starting point'.[1] And it is just this which Hare ignores when he asserts that to become morally adult is to 'learn to use "ought"-sentences in the realisation that they can only be verified by reference to a standard or set of principles which we have by our own decision accepted and made our own'.[2]

Though the difference between the views of Hare and Murphy is not, at first, very striking, it is nevertheless a fundamental one. Murphy rightly insists that if a decision is to make sense it must be founded upon values which the agent did not himself decide either to accept or reject.

> If everything in a moral situation were arguable or questionable at once, there could be no significant questioning or argument.[3]

On the other hand, Hare's reference to a set of principles 'which we have by our own decision accepted', makes it clear that he regards these values as themselves a matter for decision, and this is a radical confusion. For since there would *ex hypothesi* be no considerations in terms of which such a decision could be explained, it would simply be unintelligible – and with it any further judgement or decision founded upon it.

I say that Hare's concept of a decision is 'unintelligible' and not 'arbitrary' or 'unfounded' (as some of Hare's critics

---

[1] *The Theory of Practical Reason*, p. 195.
[2] Hare, *The Language of Morals*, p. 78.   [3] Murphy, op. cit., p. 193.

have suggested) advisedly. For even an arbitrary decision must be based on considerations in a way in which Hare's could not be. Suppose, for example, that I toss a coin or draw lots in order to decide between two alternatives A and B. It might be thought that this is a paradigm case of an unfounded decision, and in one way it is. For I could not give an answer to the question, 'Why did you choose A rather than B?' by appealing to any relevant feature of A. My choice is quite different from, say, the choice of a car because of its styling or a camera because of its lens. Nevertheless, it is not unintelligible. There are considerations in terms of which it can be understood. I can point out, for instance, that though there was no necessity for me to choose A rather than B, there were features of the situation which made it necessary for me to make some choice. And I might go on to explain how, in such a situation, a man in my society may commit himself to the outcome of tossing a coin, how he may intentionally leave things to chance. Within this social context even an arbitrary decision has a sense.

Only then, by recognising that our moral decisions and judgements are based on considerations which we did not decide to accept, but which stem from the way of life in which we were brought up, can we avoid the sort of mistake which Hare makes. In order to explain why moral decisions have such an important part to play in our lives, we must see that in making them a man is applying considerations which he has been raised to regard as of fundamental importance. In recognising this, we are making no concessions to conventionalism. We are simply rejecting one mistaken concept of a decision. Morality does not depend on decisions. On the contrary, if it means anything at all to speak of someone making a moral judgement or reaching a moral decision, this is because what he says can be understood as part of an established morality.

Conclusion

Now that I have, to the best of my ability, explained what I feel to be the main deficiencies in the accounts of moral reasoning offered by Hare and Mrs. Foot, it may seem rather late in the day to turn to questions about the nature of philosophy. Yet it is at this point that such questions naturally arise. On reading this essay, someone may be perplexed by my claim that these writers misdescribe the nature of moral reasoning. Such a reaction is quite an intelligible one. One may be inclined to ask how it is possible to give a false account of anything as familiar as morality. Surely it is easy enough to say what men are doing when they make moral judgements, or support the judgements which they have made with reasons. And if so, why do philosophers fall into error?

One answer to this question is, I think, to be found in the different ways in which a man approaches the study of human activities. Two quotations will illustrate this diversity. The first, which I believe to present a mistaken view, is taken from Vilfredo Pareto's *The Mind and Society*:

> The proposition so often met with, 'This or that people acts as it does because of a certain belief', is rarely true; in fact, it is almost always erroneous.[1]

The second which I wish to consider is to be found in Wittgenstein's *Philosophical Investigations*, and advocates

[1] *The Mind and Society*, vol. I, p. 90.

an approach diametrically opposed to that of Pareto. Wittgenstein maintains that:

> What people accept as a justification is shown by how they think and live.[1]

Now, it would be convenient if the difference between the accounts which I have criticised and my own account could without reservation be equated with the differences between these two approaches. Unfortunately, the matter is not as simple as that, for Hare and Mrs. Foot would certainly wish to reject the approach recommended by Pareto, and would probably declare their adherence to Wittgenstein's views. Nevertheless, I do not think that such an identification would be without significance, for though they may pay lip-service to Wittgenstein's views, it is only in a superficial sense that they may be said to have learned from him. Though they go some way towards trying to explain moral justification in terms of the reasons which men actually give and accept for their moral beliefs, basically their approach to human beliefs and activities is similar to Pareto's.

The reason why this is so is that both writers begin their enquiries with certain presuppositions. Instead of examining moral discourse in order to see what men count as a reason, they assume that to some extent they already know, and what does not fit in with their preconceived models they reject. Thus because Hare thinks of moral argument as a type of syllogistic inference, he is led to suppose that anything could count as a moral reason, and is then unable to explain why there are certain things which we do not regard as relevant to morality. On the other hand, Mrs. Foot, who accepts a different model, and interprets moral justification as a type of empirical justification, is unable to account for the kinds of radical disagreement which the former, but not the latter, occasions.

The fact that philosophers misdescribe things with which they are perfectly familiar, then, does not imply any severe lack of comprehension on their part. The mistakes and confusions in their accounts arise because their understand-

[1] *Philosophical Investigations*, 325, p. 106e.

Conclusion

ing has been distorted by the models which they have adopted. The result is a systematic lapse into nonsense which can be arrested only by a wholesale rejection of these models. And it is here that the maxim, 'Don't think, but look',[1] becomes important. For in order to escape from the grip of false theories, we have to stop assuming that moral reasons *must* be of a certain sort, and look to see how they actually *are* used by moral agents. This does not involve a superficial or uncritical approach to philosophy (as some writers have thought). It does imply taking seriously what men regard as a justification.

I have suggested in the preceding chapters that when we do this, there are two important things which we notice. The first is the diversity in what people count as a moral reason. Thus, the question 'Why did X do wrong?' asked of a Catholic, may elicit the answer 'X took his own life', but this is not a reason which, for example a Japanese Samurai might accept. Again, the Samurai might justify his condemnation of someone's actions in a way which would be quite unacceptable to the Catholic.

The second point is that, despite this diversity, not anything can count as a moral reason. Neither the Catholic nor the Samurai is at liberty to bring forward whatever considerations he chooses in defence of his views. What can and what cannot count as a reason is determined by the communities to which they belong.

These two points are not, I hope, the only ones to emerge from the preceding chapters. For they themselves raise many other issues on which I have tried to throw some light, and many more which are beyond the scope of this investigation. But I believe that in the present state of moral philosophy they are the most important. And though there are many points in this book of which I am still unsure, these are not among them. I am at least certain that any account of morality which emphasises either of these aspects to the exclusion of the other cannot claim to give an intelligible account of the nature of moral reasoning.

[1] *Philosophical Investigations*, 66, p. 31e.

Bibliography

Anscombe, G. E. M., 'Modern Moral Philosophy', *Philosophy*, Vol. XXXIII.
Aristotle, *Nichomachean Ethics*, trans. by J. A. K. Thompson, Penguin Classics, 1955.
Ayer, A. J., *Language, Truth and Logic*, Victor Gollancz, 1962.
Bambrough, R., 'Unanswerable Questions', *Proc. Arist. Soc. Supp.*, Vol. XL.
Bentham, Jeremy, *Introduction to the Principles of Morals and Legislation*, Oxford University Press, 1879.
Black, Max, 'The Gap Between "Is" and "Should"', *Philosophical Review*, April, 1964.
Bradley, F. H., *Ethical Studies*, Oxford University Press, 1927.
Brecht, Bertolt, 'Anmerkungen zum Lustspiel "Mann ist Mann"', *Schriften zum Theater*, Vol. 2, Suhrkamp Verlag, 1960.
Brecht, Bertolt, 'Uber eine nicht-aristotelische Dramatik', *Schriften zum Theater*, Vol. 3, Suhrkamp Verlag, 1960.
Butler, Samuel, *Earnest Pontifex, or The Way of All Flesh*, World's Classics, Oxford, 1936.
Camus, Albert, *The Outsider*, trans. by Stuart Gilbert, Penguin Modern Classics, 1961.
Camus, Albert, *The Plague*, trans. by Stuart Gilbert, Penguin Modern Classics, 1960.
Camus, Albert, *The Rebel*, trans. by Anthony Bower, Peregrine Books, 1962.
Dickens, Charles, *David Copperfield*, Chapman and Hall, 1901.
Dickens, Charles, *Hard Times*, Everyman Series, 1963.
Eysenck, H. J., *Fact and Fiction in Psychology*, Penguin Books, 1965.

Bibliography

Foot, Philippa, 'Goodness and Choice', *Proc. Arist. Soc.* Supp., Vol. XXXV.
Foot, Philippa, 'Immoralist', *New York Review of Books*, Vol. 6, Number 2.
Foot, Philippa, 'Moral Arguments', *Mind*, Vol. LXVII.
Foot, Philippa, 'Moral Beliefs', *Mind*, Vol. LIX.
Foot, Philippa, 'When is a Principle a Moral Principle?', *Proc. Arist. Soc.* Supp., Vol. XXVIII.
Frazer, Sir James George, *The Golden Bough: a Study in Magic and Religion* (Abridged Edition), Macmillan, 1923.
Geach, P. T., 'Good and Evil', *Analysis*, Vol. 17, Number 2.
Graves, Robert, *I, Claudius*, Methuen, 1962.
Greene, Graham, *Brighton Rock*, Penguin Books, 1943.
Greene, Graham, *The Heart of the Matter*, Penguin Books, 1962.
Hare, R. M., 'Descriptivism', *Proc. Brit. Acad.*, 1963.
Hare, R. M., *Freedom and Reason*, Oxford University Press, 1963.
Hare, R. M., 'Geach: Good and Evil', *Analysis*, Vol. 17, Number 3.
Hare, R. M., *The Language of Morals*, Oxford University Press, 1960.
Harrison, J., 'When is a Principle a Moral Principle?', *Proc. Arist. Soc.* Supp., Vol. XXVIII.
Hume, David, *An Enquiry Concerning Human Understanding*, ed. L. A. Selby-Bigge, Oxford University Press, 1902.
Hume, David, 'A Dialogue', *Essays: Moral, Political and Literary*, Vol. 4, Longmans, 1889.
Kierkegaard, Sören, *The Present Age*, trans. by A. Dru, Fontana, 1962.
Kierkegaard, Sören, *Purity of Heart*, trans. by D. Steere, Fontana, 1961.
Kuprin, A. I., *The Duel and Selected Stories*, trans. by A. R. MacAndrew, Signet Classics, 1961.
Malcolm, Norman, *Wittgenstein: a Memoir*, Oxford University Press, 1958.
Meager, R., 'The Impossibility of a Common Factor and the Indefinite Extendability of Reasoning About Values', *Common Factor*, Vol. 1, Number 1.
Melden, A. I., *Rights and Right Conduct*, Basil Blackwell, 1959.
Mill, J. S., 'Bentham', in *Utilitarianism*, ed. by M. Warnock, Fontana, 1962.
Mill, J. S., *Utilitarianism*, Longmans, Green and Co., 1897.
Mounce, H. O., and Phillips, D. Z., 'On Morality's Having a Point', *Philosophy*, Vol. XL, 1965.

Murphy, A. E., *The Theory of Practical Reason*, Open Court, 1964.
Nietzsche, Friedrich, *Beyond Good and Evil. Prelude to a Philosophy of the Future*, trans. by Helen Zimmern, T. N. Foulis, 1909.
Nowell-Smith, P. H., *Ethics*, Penguin Books, 1954.
Pareto, Vilfredo, *The Mind and Society*, Vol. I, Harcourt Brace, 1935.
Phillips, D. Z., and Mounce, H. O., 'On Morality's Having a Point', *Philosophy*, Vol. XL, 1965.
Piaget, Jean, *The Moral Judgement of the Child*, Routledge and Kegan Paul, 1931.
Plato, *Gorgias*, trans. by W. Hamilton, Penguin Classics, 1960.
Plato, *The Republic*, trans. by F. M. Cornford, Oxford University Press, 1955.
Popper, Karl, *The Open Society*, Vols. 1 and 2, Routledge and Kegan Paul, 1945.
Ramsey, F. P., *The Foundations of Mathematics, and other Logical Essays*, Routledge and Kegan Paul, 1931.
Rhees, R., 'Some Developments in Wittgenstein's View of Ethics', *Philosophical Review*, Vol. LXXIV, Number I.
Scott, Sir Walter, *The Heart of Midlothian*, Adam and Charles Black, 1870.
Shakespeare, W., *Measure for Measure*, Cambridge University Press, 1923.
Tolstoi, Leo N., *Anna Karenina*, trans. by R. S. Townsend, Everyman's Library, 1912.
Tolstoi, Leo N., *Resurrection*, trans. by Louise Maude, World's Classics, Oxford, 1952.
Von Wright, G. H., *The Varieties of Goodness*, Routledge and Kegan Paul, 1963.
Walsh, W. H., 'Moral Authority and Moral Choice', *Proc. Arist. Soc.*, Vol. LXV.
Weil, Simone, *The Need for Roots*, trans. by A. F. Wills, Routledge and Kegan Paul, 1952.
Williams, Tennessee, *Cat on a Hot Tin Roof*, Secker and Warburg, 1956.
Wisdom, J., *Paradox and Discovery*, Basil Blackwell, 1965.
Wittgenstein, Ludwig, *Philosophical Investigations*, trans. by G. E. M. Anscombe, Basil Blackwell, 1963.

Index

adultery, 38, 42, 43, 44, 50, 79, 121, 127–9
agreement in a form of life, 124–5
agreement in judgements, 121, 124
agreement in opinions, 124–5
Anscombe, G. E. M., xiii, 14–15, 21n., 138
arguments, empirical, *see* disagreement
  moral, *see* disagreement
  syllogistic, 4–10, 30–2, 69, 70, 71–2, 136
Aristotle, 19n., 138
art, 20–1, 126–7
Ayer, A. J., 71, 138

Bambrough, R., 113, 138
Bentham, J., 87
  Introduction to the Principles of Morals and Legislation, 108, 115, 117, 120, 138
Black Max, 72, 73, 75, 138
Bradley, F. H., 122–3, 131, 138
breakdowns, moral, x, 11, 75, 105, 109, 117–18
Brecht, B., 20, 138
Butler, S., 87, 138

Caligula, 33
Camus, A., *The Outsider*, 29, 99–100, 138
  The Plague, 88–9, 138
  The Rebel, 62, 138
cannibalism, 46–8
capital punishment, 48n., 88–9
Catholic morality, 72, 76, 77, ch. 8 *passim*, 121–2, 137
causal relationship, xiv

charity, 44
Chekhov, A. P., 39, 62
chess, 72–6
Christ, 54
'closed society', 111–12
'competent judges', 89–90
conventionalism, 56, ch. 10 *passim*
conversion, 90–1
courage, 14, 44, 45, 47, 62, 68–9

Descartes, 87
decisions, 31, 32, 33, 79, 80, 100, 122, 123, 124, 131, 132–4
decisions of principle, 80
Dickens, C., *David Copperfield*, 57–8, 60, 138
  Hard Times, 87, 138
disagreement, aesthetic, x, 20–1
  empirical, x, xv, 11, 104–10
  mathematical, 86
  moral, ix, x, xv, part II *passim*
diversity of moral standards, xiv, ch. 4 *passim*, 137

economics, x
emotivism, 71, 96
etiquette, xi, 13
existentialism, xi
'experts' in morality, 88–9
Eysenck, H. J., 52–3, 139

family, the, 9, 110–11, 115, 132
Foot, P., 'Goodness and Choice', xiii, 11, 18, 19, 27, 139
  'Immortalist', 59, 139
  'Moral Arguments', xiii, 11, 12, 13, 16, 109, 139

Foot, P.—*continued*
  'Moral Beliefs', xiii, 11, 14, 15, 21, 69, 139
  'When is a Principle a Moral Principle?', 11, 40n., 139
Frazer, Sir J. G., 47, 139
Freud, S., 63
functional words, 18

Geach, P. T., xiii, 18, 26, 139
'good and harm', 14, 17, 21, 22, 71, 115, 116
Graves, R., 33, 139
greed, 42, 95, 101
Greene, G., *Brighton Rock*, 102–3, 139
  The Heart of the Matter, 72, 76, 94, 139
guilt, 50–3

happiness, 21
hara-kiri, 33
Hare, R. M., 'Descriptivism', 48, 139
  Freedom and Reason, xi, 3, 4, 30, 40, 46, 93, 98–9, 122, 139
  The Language of Morals, xi, xii, 3, 4, 6, 7, 8, 25, 28, 32, 68, 70, 96, 122, 123–4, 126, 139
Harrison, J., 49–53, 139
Hegel, 123
Hippocratic Oath, 6
history, x, 113–14
'human flourishing', 14, 21
Hume, D., *An Enquiry Concerning Human Understanding*, xiv, 139
  'A Dialogue', 37–8, 44–5, 139
humility, 44, 55, 57, 58, 59, 60
hypocrisy, 58–60, 127

injury, 21–3
insight, moral, 87–91, 132
integrity, 9, 42, 43, 44, 60, 83, 88

Jehovah's Witness, the, 22
justice, 14, 17, 83, 85, 87

Kierkegaard, S., 54
  Purity of Heart, 129–30, 139
  The Present Age, 56, 139

learning a skill, 96
learning from experience, 87–91
Lorre, Peter, 20
lying, 7, 8, 9, 80, 95, 96–7, 98, 131

Mafiosi, 40
Malcolm, N., 22, 139
'mentally ill', 99
Mill, J. S., 'Bentham', 87, 139
  Utilitarianism, 15, 89n., 90, 139
monk, the, 39, 62
Moore, G. E., 22
'moral beliefs', 81–7
moral instruction, 86, 122–3, 133,
Mounce, H. O., 13n., 124n., 139
murder, 29, 31, 38, 41, 42, 43, 44, 49, 50, 79, 80, 86, 87, 88–9, 95, 98, 99–100, 112
Murphy, A. E., 133, 140

Nazis, 29, 40
Nietzsche, F., ch. 5 *passim*, 140
Nowell-Smith, P. H., xi, 140

'ordinary language', 102

Pareto, V., 135–6, 140
Phillips, D. Z., 13n., 140
Piaget, J., 97, 140
piety, 55
Plato, *Gorgias*, 60, 140
  Republic, 57, 140
pleasure, 21
pleasure principle, the, 13, 115
Popper, K. R., xi, 31, 111–12, 140
prejudice, 83
principles, 4, 8, 80–7
promise-keeping, 98
propaganda, x

Ramsey, F. P., 24, 140
rationalisation, 6
rebel, the, 38–9, ch. 5 *passim*
remorse, 49–53
revolutionary, the, *see* rebel
Rhees, R., viii, 17, 140
'rude', 13

Samurai, the, 137
science, x, 63, 64, 106–7, 115
Scott, Sir Walter, 41, 140
self-evidence, 15–16
self-interest, 21, 43, 59
self-sacrifice, 44
Shakespeare, W., 110–11, 112, 115, 140
Sloan, Tod, 83
Solomon, R. L., 52
solution to a moral dispute, 104–6
  to a moral problem, 108–9, 110–19

Index

solution—*continued*
    to an empirical dispute, 104–6, 110–19
stamp-collecting, 35
status quo, 63
suffering, 88–9, 107
suicide, 42–4, 72, 76, 79, 92–5, 101–3, 121

temperance, 68–9
Tolstoi, L., 54
    Anna Karenina, 126–9, 140
    Resurrection, 118–19, 140
truth-telling, 42, 44, 55, 79, 80

understanding an alien morality, 35–6, 45
utilitarianism, xii, 56, 90, 108, 117

vivisection, 106–8, 117
Von Wright, G. H., 15, 140

Walsh, W. H., 79–80, 140
Weil, S., 55, 140
Williams, Tennessee, 6, 140
Wisdom, J., 83n., 140
Wittgenstein, Ludwig, viii, 22, 121, 124–5, 135–7, 140

For Product Safety Concerns and Information please contact our EU
representative GPSR@taylorandfrancis.com
Taylor & Francis Verlag GmbH, Kaufingerstraße 24, 80331 München, Germany

www.ingramcontent.com/pod-product-compliance
Lightning Source LLC
Chambersburg PA
CBHW071940240426
43669CB00048B/2475